START RIGHT.
END RIGHT.

This book is dedicated to
Ted Forcht
1960-2019

START RIGHT. END RIGHT.

The Terry Forcht Story

by Gary P. West & Eddie Woodruff

Foreword by U.S. Senator Mitch McConnell

Acclaim Press
MORLEY, MISSOURI

Acclaim Press
—— *Your Next Great Book* ——

P.O. Box 238
Morley, MO 63767
(573) 472-9800
www.acclaimpress.com

Book Design: Rayla B. Trigg
Cover Design: Derek Melvin
Editorial Review: Jill Amelung
Special thanks to Florence Huffman and Mark Green for conducting interviews
for this book.

ISBN: 978-1-948901-39-0 | 1-948901-39-0
Library of Congress Control Number: 2019953251
First Printing 2020
Printed in the United States of America
10 9 8 7 6 5 4 3 2 1

This publication was produced using available information.
The publisher regrets it cannot assume responsibility for errors or omissions.

Contents

Foreword

ℰ)ℭ

When Terry asked me if I would add a few thoughts of my own to the book that follows, I was delighted not only to learn that he was putting down on paper the story of his remarkable career up to now, but also delighted to oblige. As one who represents all Kentuckians in Washington, it is a true honor for me to pay tribute to a man who has done so much for so many citizens of the Commonwealth.

As I write, our nation is passing through a period full of challenges and uncertainty. Many Americans are wondering for the first time in their lives whether their children will have the same opportunities they did; or, to put it another way, whether they will leave America better off than they found it. In the midst of all these concerns, the only right response is the one that Terry Forcht lives every day: a life of hard work, unshakeable principles, respect for others, and a firm belief in the enduring greatness of America.

Terry's life contains many lessons, and not only for those who wish to succeed in business. For young couples, Terry and Marion show how a true partnership can multiply one's efforts. Terry's work ethic can serve as a model for motivating others in any undertaking. His legendary focus could be used to train athletes and students as well as boardroom executives. And his involvement in his community, whether it's at Grace on the Hill Church in Corbin, educational institutions like the University of the Cumberlands or the University of Louisville, or his work in preserving our Kentucky heritage through improvements to the State Capitol in Frankfort, is a worthy model for Kentuckians of every stripe.

Of particular note in this regard is the tremendous contribution Terry has made through the Excellence in Leadership Program at the University of the Cumberlands. To the extent that this program was inspired in some way by the McConnell Center at the University of Louisville, I am proud to have played a part in its conception. Helping to cultivate the next generation of leaders in the Commonwealth has always been a top priority for me. I know it is a top priority for Terry as well. I commend him for his generous efforts in this area.

As someone who interacts regularly with leaders in industry and finance, two things stand out right away about Terry. First of all, he makes no apologies for being a conservative Republican. He believes in his core that the Party of Lincoln represents the best direction for the Commonwealth and the nation, and he doesn't mind letting people know it. Most prominent businessmen play both sides of the political fence in an effort to hedge themselves in the event that one party falls out of favor. Not Terry. He stands for what he believes in both in season and out of season. I assure you, this is a rare and admirable trait.

It is this same willingness to go against the grain that enabled Terry to believe early on in his career that he could succeed by starting out not in the big city, but in rural markets others had overlooked. That insight, along with his willingness to partner with people from whom he thought he could learn about the various businesses in which he is now involved, are a testament to his daring and creative approach. Like other great leaders, Terry always knew what he didn't know and surrounded himself with people from whom he could learn. It's a model that goes back at least as far as

Terry's successful partnership with our departed friend and former Republican National Committeewoman, Nelda Barton Collings. Years later, it is clear from the respect he shows his employees that he still thinks he has much to learn from others.

Another secret of Terry's success is his determination to be the hardest working employee on his staff. According to Terry, you simply cannot expect someone on your staff to do something you're not willing to do yourself. Put another way, you can't expect to get more from your employees than you're willing to give yourself. That's why Terry works seven days a week, and that's also why he is known to travel with multiple cell phones. If one carrier drops a call during his daily travels around Kentucky, there is always another phone handy that uses a different carrier. This is just one of the tricks Terry employs to stay on top of businesses that range from radio to retail and to ensure that no detail of his complex and multi-layered business holdings escapes his attention.

Terry's employees not only know they need to be available at all times, they also know that everyone associated with the Forcht Group is expected to maintain a strict open-door policy. How strict? Well, legend has it that one employee who resisted the idea arrived at work one day to find the door to his office had been removed from its hinges. He didn't have to be told after that how strict the policy was taken at the Forcht Group. It's a policy that Terry applies just as strictly to himself.

Much is made of the fact that Terry has built an extensive business empire across the Commonwealth. It is, without doubt, an astonishing feat. But to many of us, even more impressive than Terry's ability to manage some ninety-three different businesses is his ability to do it all without losing any of the humility that has always marked his private and public persona. Despite all the demands on his time, Terry does not think twice about picking up the phone to personally recommend a young student who could use a boost in life. He is also well known for treating everyone on his staff with interest and concern.

Over the years, I have been fortunate enough to earn Terry's political support, and I am grateful for it. In fact, after watching how hard Terry works on behalf of the candidates he supports and how persuasive he can be, one can't help but wonder whether he could have had an equally successful career in politics. It should be obvious at this point that I have great respect for Terry not only for his incredible achievements in business, but also as a man. He is a model Kentuckian and, indeed, a model American. It is my hope that through the telling of his story, he inspires many more Kentuckians to blaze the kind of trail he has. They will find all the tools they need by studying the life and example of Terry Forcht.

U.S. Senator Mitch McConnell
Louisville, Kentucky

Introduction

✂︎)(✂︎

There might not be another man in America…or perhaps the world…that is as focused, structured and driven as Terry E. Forcht. His life is his work.

Normal people work five days a week. But, nothing about Terry is normal. Never has been. Never will be. He works the usual five, plus Saturday, and then a half-day on Sunday, not because he has to, but because he wants to.

He reached senior citizen status several years ago, but he still embarks on a daily routine of which few teenagers could keep pace: a 3:30 a.m. wake-up; eats breakfast; walks the dog; 5:30 a.m. arrives at corporate office number one in Corbin; feeds the cat; makes coffee; writes notes to staff; 6:45 a.m. departs for corporate office number two in Lexington; twenty-two phone calls in route; 8 a.m. arrival in Lexington. Now he's ready to get to work.

Terry's life has spanned being a part of the last generation climbing out of the Depression who can remember the impact of a world at war that rattled the structure of daily lives for years.

He grew up in the era of ration books for everything from gas to sugar to shoes to stoves. Milk was delivered to front porches and placed in a milk box. Boys came home from the war and built little houses … lots of them. Childhoods were spent without TV. Instead, people pictured in their minds what they heard on radio. There was a single phone in the home with a "party line" shared by others.

Parents became free from the restraints of the Depression and the war, and they threw themselves into exploring opportunities they had never imagined. Children weren't neglected, but they weren't today's all-consuming family focus either. They were glad their kids played by themselves until the streetlights came on.

Their kids began to feel secure in their future, and Terry Forcht was among them. He knew, even at a young age, he wanted to do more with his life than just take up space. And has he ever.

He has lived most of his life out of the limelight in Corbin, Kentucky, at the foothills of the Cumberland Mountains. His low profile and quiet personality have permitted him and his wife, Marion, to enjoy life without much hassle.

While the Forcht name (pronounced fork) is well known in eastern Kentucky, Lexington, northern Kentucky, and somewhat in Louisville, in the rest of the state, not as much.

Terry's entrepreneurial skills have resulted in nine nursing homes, twenty-six banking locations, twenty-five radio stations, twenty finance company offices, two newspapers, and three insurance companies. There's more, but who's counting.

Born Terry Emanuel Forcht at Norton Hospital in Louisville on April 28, 1938, he has long been on a mission to succeed. He accomplished that years ago.

"He believes the reason most people don't recognize opportunity when it knocks," says wife Marion, "is because it's usually disguised as hard work."

For Terry Forcht life is a journey, not a destination, and for the scores of people who have taken that trip with him, they have been rewarded. He has created thirteen millionaires within his organization. Their trustworthiness has permitted him to delegate, which means a path to growing his company. Through his start-ups and acquisitions, he has often been described as a deal maker, and to a point a risk taker. He is both. And his charitable work is legendary.

This is the story of a man who has amassed a business empire based on building one company on top of another.

It goes something like this: Nursing home residents need prescriptions, so he starts a pharmacy. Banks and nursing homes need furniture, so there's a retail furniture store in Lexington. A bank needs to advertise, so there are radio stations and newspapers. Someone has to build them, so he has a construction company. They all need insurance, so guess what, he has an insurance company. It's what Terry calls "inter-company business". There's more, but by now you get the picture.

Terry has surrounded himself with like-minded people. It is essential they have a work ethic that, though it may not be able to match his, is at least in the same neighborhood. These individuals also need to be trustworthy.

Those who meet these criteria have reached the upper echelon and are deemed to be group leaders of the multiple companies owned by Terry Forcht that has evolved into The Forcht Group of Kentucky.

What motivates this man? What keeps his business edge razor sharp? What keeps him true to himself? He doesn't have to look far.

"It's the success of building one company and then being able to get into a new venture," he says. "We build one company on top of another."

For Terry, the small towns of Kentucky offer more of a human connection with others. And his business world has been conducted mostly in these small towns. Forcht Group has maintained these small-town values at the heart of the company's success.

"Most people want to leave home and go to the big cities and find opportunities," says Terry. "I came from a big city to a small town. It seems to have worked out pretty good for me."

While some see a glass as half full or half empty, it doesn't surprise anyone who has ever known Terry Forcht that he sees the glass full to the brim.

✦

START RIGHT.
END RIGHT.

The Terry Forcht Story

Chapter One

Early Entrepreneur

ℰℴℛ

G rowing up at 1482 Olive Street in Louisville, there was nothing that would have predicted Terry Forcht would become an entrepreneurial genius. No one ever knows for sure what's inside a person.

They are all around us, those that should be successful in life, but aren't. And, then there are those with their heart-felt stories of overcoming all odds to reach a level of unexpected success.

Success is measured in many different ways: lots of friends, a good job, a big house, a fine car, and fancy clothes. To some, they work all their lives and don't attain any of these, while others work all their lives and attain them all. It's difficult to say what makes one person more successful than another. Sociologists have studied it for decades. But for Terry Forcht, he knows success when he sees it, and he has seen it in increments all his life.

His father, Emanuel, and his mother, Evelyn, were married in 1935, and his father worked for $60 a week at Kroger Grocery and Bakery. The couple rented an apartment on South 38th Street for $25 a month before moving to Brookline Avenue a year later. Their rent was $17 a month.

Being of German descent, Manuel (this is what Evelyn called him) was always trying to better his lot in life, and in January 1938 they purchased a little four-room house at 1482 Olive Street for $3,900. Three months later Terry E. Forcht was born.

The Forcht family's commitment to each other, to their family, and to their neighborhood provided a nurturing environment for raising Terry and his younger sister, Janey.

After ten years at Kroger, Terry's dad decided on a career change by selling insurance. He hated it, and a year later he was back in the grocery business working at a couple of neighborhood markets. The Forchts were doing their best to keep ahead.

"In my opinion, they were more successful than any millionaires I know," says Terry in talking about his parents. "They knew how to have a home full of love, and they knew how to be happy. They were rich in peace of mind."

How many times have you heard about a talented athlete that couldn't or wouldn't convert his ability to become a superstar? On the other hand, next to him might be an athlete, shorter or slower who would be the best player on the team. We've seen it a hundred times.

Why? It's something hard to define, but easy to say with just one word: Desire. Not everyone has it, and it doesn't just pertain to sports. It can be seen in every walk of life.

Desire has to be something we are born with that releases a chemical into the heart and brain at different stages of life. It can't be taught in a classroom or coached on a field. Yes, it can be preached from the pulpit or discussed in a motivational seminar, but if there's not a "deep-inside-you" undefinable, unexplainable mechanism urging you on, then it may not matter. Terry Forcht is a living example of the definition of desire.

He didn't know he had it as a young boy. In fact, he didn't know what he really wanted to do. It seemed like he always had something going on, not necessarily a job, but things that were expected of him from his mother and father.

For any young boy growing up in the '50s, a bicycle was his main mode of getting around. With a mom and dad working six days a week, there was little time to haul their kids around. During that era Louisville was considered a safe place, with less traffic and less crime, and with only a couple of television stations to watch (what kid in Louisville didn't want to be on T-Bar-V with Randy and Cactus?).

There were days of summer when Terry and several of his friends would find their way to Fontaine Ferry Park, a West End amusement venue that drew kids and adults from across Louisville and surrounding towns to its huge swimming pool, skating rink and Hilarity Hall. To Louisvillian's it was called Fountain Ferry, and it seemed like every other day the park had a promotion going on. A certain number of bottle caps from soft drinks could gain free admittance, or a certain number of labels from almost anything could get you free ride tickets. It was fun and Terry enjoyed his trips there.

He also relishes the memories of Algonquin Park, where he spent much of his time with neighborhood kids. "It was a great place to be with friends," Terry says. "It had a wading pool, a playground, and some ball fields where we'd play baseball or anything else. It's where we socialized and got to really know each other." One of Terry's boyhood friends, Bill Underwood, was known for a unique talent — he could recite the alphabet backwards. Brothers Tom & L.G. Owen lived three doors down from the Forchts and once had a contest with Terry to see who could collect the most bottle caps. (Tom Owen has worked as an archivist and historian at the University of Louisville since 1968. He also served on the Louisville city council for over 20 years.)

Manual and Evelyn were not much into permitting their children to just sit around in the house. "Get outside, find something to do," they would say in a not so calm voice. And if you were sick, well, you really had to be sick. "If you feel sick in the morning, go to school anyway," Terry remembers being told. "And if you are really sick, they'll send you home, and then it's okay."

Doc Green lived near Olive Street, and there would be times the Forcht kids made a visit to the office at his house."If something hurt, Mom would say, 'give it a week,'" Terry laughed. "If it still hurt after that, we'd go see Doc Green."

McFarren Grade School was close to the Forcht's home, and like the nearby city park, it was a place where he learned to respect the authority of his teachers and the responsibility of class work. He figured out quickly that this school thing was long term.

By his own admission he was an average student. "I struggled with spelling, and still do to this day," said Terry. But he also knew that what he learned at McFarren Grade School, and later Parkland Junior High, would hopefully serve him well when he reached high school.

In the West End, sidewalks that went somewhere ran in front of the houses. Within walking distance or an easy bike ride were grocery stores, beauty shops, drugstores, and even a corner tavern. This is what neighborhoods in Louisville were all about in the 1940s and '50s.

Front porches were where neighbors on Olive Street socialized. In the summer it was not unusual to see folks sitting out front in a comfortable chair with a fan in hand well after dark. Home air conditioning was a luxury that had not yet arrived in the West End. They knew everyone who walked or drove by. Backyard barbecues had not yet come into vogue, and neither had fences. Neighbors in the West End were actually neighborly. This was the Forcht family's world.

Louisville had always been a neighborhood town, and each had their own identity as well as their own little newspapers. In no way did they compete with the morning Courier-Journal or afternoon Louisville Times, but the West End News had its own niche, and one of Terry's first jobs while still in junior high was making sure every Thursday afternoon he delivered his 400 papers. At 20 cents per hundred, the 80 cents fee he made was just one of several revenue streams he was engaged in. And this was back when a dollar was really a dollar.

He didn't know it at the time, but he was just getting his feet wet in becoming an entrepreneur. For sure he couldn't spell it, but for certain he was making money several different ways.

Besides the paper delivery, Terry hunted night crawlers at the schoolyard. He'd fill up a coffee can and sell it to fishermen and bait shops for a dollar. "I could stick a flashlight in my mouth, aim it at the ground, and bring out the night crawlers," he said. "These sales were all profit, with no investment, just a little time."

Then there were the pencils. Vendors at his dad's market would give him pencils, and he would bring them home to Terry, who would then take them to school and sell them for a penny less than his classmates could buy them at school. No cost, 100% profit. What a country!

He also went to the A & P Grocery Store and bought cartons of chewing gum at 80 cents each. With 120 sticks of gum in each carton, he sold them at a penny each – 40 cents profit per carton. Not bad for a budding entrepreneur.

"Chewing gum was big back then," Terry laughed. "It seemed like everyone was chewing gum, so I sold all I had at bus stops. I was always selling something, and at times I'd sell candy. But, I had strict orders not to eat any of it. My mom wouldn't even let me eat candy at Easter. I do, however, remember my first candy bar, a Heath Bar. Selling was my family's background. I learned how to sell and stayed with it." Did he ever!

A bit later Terry delivered prescriptions on his bike. First, it was Sherman Drugs at 18th and Market, and later at Dixon Drugs.

Terry Forcht didn't just always have a job...he had three or four. In the summers he mowed grass, mostly in the neighborhood, and when he was a little older he joined his sister, mom and dad by working concession stands at several of Louisville's city parks. One summer they would be at Shawnee, the next at Algonquin, and then another at Iroquois.

In 1955, his dad, called Gus or Manny by his customers and friends, had a chance to purchase the neighborhood market where he worked. He paid $2,000 for the business that did not include the land, and soon Manuel's Market on Woodland Avenue in the West End of Louisville was making the grocery a family enterprise.

It was a good decision. There was a solid clientele of customers, and with the entire family pitching in, their business was prosperous. Janey would come to the grocery after school at Parkland Junior High and Terry would come to help out from Shawnee High.

The work he did for his dad at Manuel's Market, like dusting, stocking shelves, cleaning out meat cases, sweeping the floors, and picking up trash, well, those were freebies. That's what kids did for their parents. He was smart enough to realize it was part of the blueprint of living in a loving home.

Terry's Tips
for Entrepreneurs

"Find your niche.
Do something you really enjoy."

Chapter Two
School & Work

❦❧

F or any eleven or twelve-year-old boy, transportation, getting around, was vital. And Terry's bicycle was just about the most valued thing he had in his possession.

He peddled over to one of the nearby shopping centers one afternoon to look around. When he came out of one of the stores his bike was gone.

"It was a big crisis in the family," Terry said. "I wasn't sure what I was going to do. My granddad was a carpenter at the Brown Hotel, and when he got off work he came over to our house and gave me two 20-dollar bills to buy a bike. I bought a Schwinn, and I'll never forget it."

His granddad also built Terry and Janey a playhouse in the backyard of their Olive Street home. According to a diary kept by Terry's mother, "Terry was always the boss of the club … the hirer and firer." He was only eight years old.

Terry's upbringing on Olive Street allowed him to know what time it was by hearing the shrill whistles that signaled shift changes and lunch hours from nearby factories.

Many families in the neighborhood shared a phone line with others. To even place a call, a central operator had to make the connection. Dial phones were still in the future. And believe it or not, until 1950, mail was delivered twice daily.

Of course, growing up in the '40s and '50s meant being aware of certain diseases, some of which had no known cure. One of those was polio, a crippling illness that every family across the nation feared. Louisville was no exception.

"I recall one boy I knew wore something around his neck that was supposed to ward off the disease," Terry said. "Polio was a concern for everyone. It was several years later before the vaccine was discovered that prevented it."

Terry's grandparents lived within walking distance of the Forcht's home on Olive Street, so their influence with Terry and sister Janey was important as their young lives began to take shape.

"My grandmother, Elizabeth Pfanmoeller (Evelyn's mother) was a huge influence," explained Terry. "She taught me about giving back … about tithing at church. From the first money I made I felt it was important to tithe."

Manuel and Evelyn Forcht may not have gone to church all the time, but they made sure that Terry and his sister at least got to Sunday School. And it was two of his Sunday School teachers who left a lasting impression on him. "Miss Margie and Miss Moneypenny were wonderful," says Terry. "But they were really against any of us going to the movies. They said movies were a bad influence on us and 'you're not sure what you'll see if you go.'"

Terry also got a dose of religion and patriotism in his grade school classes.

"It was common practice, the Bible, prayer and pledge," he said. "There was also Bible study some days after school at someone's house."

Terry's parents, because of their work schedules, didn't get to see him at any of the ball games he played in the local Little League, but he remembered playing in a "big deal" game that they did attend.

"Shively had a lighted Little League field and they got to see me pitch," he said. "I was not particularly a big kid, so I played sports that fit me—baseball and tennis."

As he got a little older, Terry upgraded from his Schwinn bike to a Doodle Bug Scooter. Although nondescript, it was not quite a motorbike, at least not a high end one.

Terry rode his scooter everywhere, always avoiding the police. Kids didn't need a driver's license to operate one, but still he didn't want to get in trouble with the police, and heaven forbid, get a ticket and lose his transportation. Not long after, he was able to upgrade to a Cushman Eagle, a top-of-the-line motor scooter.

By now he was attending Shawnee High School. Although it was a city bus ride, with one transfer away, Shawnee was where most of the West End kids went to school. "We all could have gone to Male or Manual," Terry said. "But we all liked Shawnee because it was more of a neighborhood school and we were all friends." Even today, the Shawnee High School Class of '56 holds an annual reunion in Louisville.

Sandy's Thrifty Food Market on Preston Street in the Audubon Park area provided Terry with a nice Saturday income from bagging groceries and making deliveries. And while working there, he learned a lesson from Buffalo that he never forgot.

"Buffalo, that's what we called him, was one of the older stock boys and baggers at Sandy's," said Terry. "He had been there long enough to really know the customers and who the good tippers were. If I was sacking groceries and Buffalo would see one of those big tippers, he'd find a way to nudge me out, so he could take over."

Perhaps Buffalo's strategic move was a lesson on how important good timing is, and added to Terry's strong work ethic, he was determined to learn from others.

This was a time in his life that he realized how glad he was that he had not only earned money, but saved it, too. He learned the value of a dollar from his mother. He had watched her put money in several envelopes each month: one marked for house payment, one for utilities, one for food, another for clothing, and even one for vacation.

In a way, he did something similar.

Avery Savings and Loan promoted a savings program to attract customers by "selling" shares weekly at ten cents each.

"It was my Avery Book," says Terry. "My whole family did it for years. Almost everything I made would go into my Avery Book. When I got married in 1959, I had over $5,000 in it."(About $44,000 in today's dollars.)

When Terry turned 16 in 1954, he bought his first car, a black 1950 Ford convertible with a leaky top.

"My dad was always a Chevy man," he said. "But I've always liked Fords, and that 1950 Ford was the car to have. I put one of those "ooga-horns" on it. A cop came up to the car one time and I blew the horn. He wasn't very impressed, reached inside and yanked the horn out."

Now that he had graduated from his Cushman motor scooter to a real car, he was ready to start dating … real dating.

For several years Terry had known Marion Cecil, a pretty girl of German descent, who lived with her parents, William and Gladys on Cypress Street, not far from the Forcht home. The Cecils had relatives on Olive Street, so frequently Marion and her two sisters, Beverly Ann and Linda Sue, visited the Forchts as well.

Terry and Marion had virtually grown up together, attending the same church, the same grade school, junior high, and, for a time the same high school. It wasn't until he turned 16, and bought his first car, that the two of them had their first official date. They were a cool couple in his custom V8 Ford that cost Terry $750.

That same year, 1954, Marion's family moved across Louisville to the East End. No longer a Shawnee High School girl, Terry would, as often as he could, drive across town to pick her up after school at Atherton High School. He'd hit the ooga horn pedal on the floorboard of his car just to let her know he had arrived. Half of Atherton High School knew it, including the school's principal.

"That horn was so loud," says Marion. "The principal chased him away once or twice for doing it."

Terry Forcht's reputation for selling things had already been established. But early in 1955, he did one of the biggest selling jobs in his life when he persuaded his parents to move to the East End, too.

The two teenagers, who had been "going steady" now for several months, once again, lived only a couple of blocks from each other.

How in the world could a young boy, not even out of high school, talk his parents into leaving a home they had paid $3,900 for back in the '30s and move? They were leaving a neighborhood where they knew everyone by their first name, and everyone knew theirs.

There were so many memories in the house on Olive Street. It was one of those "shotgun" houses. A shot could be fired through the front door and the buckshot could pass through every room before exiting the back door. No one knows for sure if anyone ever tried it.

The house was typical for its era, a 30-foot-wide lot and a small yard on each side of the house, an alley in the back with a garage. And in one corner of the yard was a small chicken house. They weren't there for eating, but instead for the eggs. They would all have the memories of eating their mother's German cooking in their small kitchen.

"We ate good, and usually healthy," Terry said. "Mom would fix sauerkraut, pork, spinach, and kale. Dad was a butcher, so he'd bring home fresh cuts of meat, and fresh vegetables from the store."

And how could anyone forget the stories of their grandmother shooting the squirrels out of her apricot tree. Terry never would. With a lifetime of memories, the Forchts were moving on up to the East End.

Marion Forcht offered that there was a simple reason Terry's parents moved. "Terry had a way with his folks."

"It wasn't all that difficult," he said. "I told them the neighborhood was changing and it was time to move."

Even though they had moved, Terry continued at Shawnee High School, and his dad still operated Manuel's Market on Woodland Avenue.

Terry tolerated high school academically, because he knew it was the means to an end. He had his ups and downs, and one of those downs happened when he became so frustrated with his German class, he threw the book out the window. Pulling a stunt like that brought his mother to the high school. The principal told her that in doing things like this "he's not going to amount to much."

Evelyn Forcht emphatically assured the principal that he was wrong. "Oh yes he will," she told him. "Because he's going to college."

Terry's Tips
for Entrepreneurs

"Decide on your goals, write them down, and develop a plan to reach them."

Terry's boyhood home at 1482 Olive Street, Louisville, KY.

Terry's christening in 1938. Pictured L-R: Terry's uncle and aunt Art and Wilma Brady, and parents Evelyn and Manuel Forcht.

Terry's parents, Manuel and Evelyn, on their wedding day in 1935.

Terry's best baseball stance in 1944 at age 6.

*Terry's dad and grandparents, Manuel Forcht,
and Elizabeth and Edward Pfanmoeller.*

Terry and his bike in 1947, age 9.

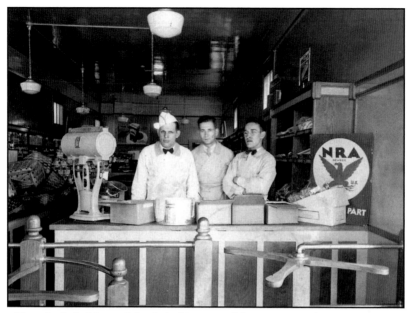

Terry's dad, Manuel (right), 23-year-old Manager of Piggly Wiggly store in 1934.

Terry, left, age 12, with neighborhood friends Stanton Skarman, Donnie Webster, and Tom Underwood.

Terry and his sister Janey, Palm Sunday, 1952.

Terry in his convertible in 1954, age 16.

The entrance to Fontaine Ferry Park in Louisville.

The Kroger store in Louisville where Terry's father worked.

Terry and Marion graduate from the University of Louisville, 1959.

Terry's MBA graduation from the University of Miami in 1961.

A 1970's photo of Terry and Marion's children at Cave Hill Cemetery in Louisville. Pictured L-R: Laurie, Debbie, Ted, and Brenda.

The Forcht family in 1978.
Standing, L-R: Marion, Terry, and Ted.
Seated: Laurie, Debbie, and Brenda.

Terry's grade school in Louisville — J.B. McFerran.

*Terry's church in Louisville — Presbyterian Church
on Woodland Ave.*

Terry's nursing homes partner, Dr. Harold Barton.

Joe Patrick, Terry's first partner.

*Terry Forcht, Debbie Reynolds, and Nelda Barton
at Wolfe County Nursing Home in 1991.*

*Tri-County National Bank Board of Directors in 1985.
L-R: Melvin Tate, John Stansberry, Avery Perry, Donald Ashley,
Chuck Rapier, Dr. Ben Wilson, Terry Forcht,
Nelda Barton, and Jim Gatlin.*

Terry, Debbie, and Hazard Nursing Home staff celebrate winning Facility of the Year in 1989.

Terry's long-time assistant, Linda Loudermelt.

Nelda Barton and Terry Forcht.

Wolfe County Nursing Home Dedication in 1991.

Ribbon cutting at Tri-County National Bank in 2000.

Ted and Jennifer Forcht wedding in 2007.

*Terry receives an honorary doctorate from the
University of the Cumberlands in 2005.*

*Wolfe County Health
& Rehabilitation
Center Winning
Facility of the Year
in 2015.
L-R: Amy Prater,
Debbie Reynolds,
Terry Forcht, and
Susan Arnold.*

WSIP Ribbon Cutting in Paintsville in 2008.

*U.K. President Dr. Eli Capilouto, Terry Forcht,
and Lexington attorney Terry McBrayer.*

Chapter Three
College & Family

℘)Ⅽℛ

E ven though Manuel and Evelyn Forcht didn't have a college education, it was always assumed their children would.

"I can still hear my daddy saying, 'Education, that's something they can't take away from you'. I really had no idea what college was about, but I grew up thinking I'd be going there," said Terry.

He had graduated from Shawnee High School as an average student in 1956, and Marion graduated from Atherton that same year. It surprised no one that they both enrolled at the University of Louisville when fall came around.

But before he headed off to college, Terry and a couple of his buddies, Vernal Huffines and Tom Kurtz, headed to Florida by way of Mississippi to make a little spending money.

"We dropped off a few dogs there," recalled Terry. "I know we got paid for it."

From Mississippi the three made their way to Miami to visit Terry's aunt and uncle, Wilma and Charles Brady. "On the way back home, I bought one of those baby alligators at Gator Land, a roadside tourist place," Terry recalled.

At the time Terry's mother, Evelyn, wrote in a diary that he put it in their bathtub and when she saw it, the alligator scared her half to death. "I don't know what she finally did with it," Terry laughed.

Marion's dad worked for DuPont Chemical Company in Louisville, and the company offered a work program for employees' children who were enrolled in college. They were paid wages of a full-time employee, and the money earned was to go toward their education expenses.

Terry still had some of his prescription delivery jobs going, and on Saturday's he continued to work at Sandy's Market. The dollars he earned helped pay his way to U of L.

He had a good experience in high school with a bookkeeping class he took. In fact, it was one of the few classes that really piqued his interest. So, at U of L he decided he would major in commerce. In 1953, the college had implemented a designated School of Business, so Terry's timing for college couldn't have been much better.

Yes, sort of like ole Buffalo over at Sandy's Market, timing his grocery sacking to get the big tips, Terry now had a firsthand experience at good timing. And it wouldn't be the last.

Don't get the impression that Terry and Marion were bookworms, doing nothing but studying, eating and sleeping—they still found time to enjoy college life, even though both lived at home.

Terry joined the Phi Kappa Tau fraternity and Marion the Kappa Delta sorority, and not much later Terry gave Marion his fraternity pin, indicating they were pinned. Being "pinned" was a bump up from going steady and a notch below being engaged. Several months later they took the next step.

They did the party thing some, but didn't overdo it. That wasn't their style. Terry wasn't above an occasional beer every now and then. After all, how could you be German and not like beer? When they were younger, he and sister Janey had stopped off at the Volcano Bar and Hemlock Cafe' with their dad, where he had a beer after work. "Kids were allowed to go in these neighborhood bars with their parents back then," said Terry.

As he and Marion continued dating, he never lost sight of the finish line. Terry accelerated his efforts toward a college degree. It was a common practice for Terry to stay up all night studying. He was an oddity in that he could function at a high level with little sleep. That ability would serve him well down the road.

Overloaded with classes every semester, he still worked jobs here and there that included being a part-time bank teller at Royal Bank in Louisville. It was here that Terry got some more advice.

"An old teller told me that when I cashed a check, I'd better know how to go out and collect it if it was bad," he recalled. "I'd always call upstairs to the office before I turned over any money."

Just three years after enrolling at U of L, Terry E. Forcht, in the spring of 1959, walked in the commencement ceremony and received a bachelor's degree in business administration. His grades had been outstanding, and along the way he had been named the "Outstanding Management Student" at U of L, an honor that came with a $100 award – real money in those days!

His mother, Evelyn, had been right when she told the principal at Shawnee High that her son was, indeed, going to amount to something, because he was going to college.

"I had only finished my junior year, but Terry wanted me to go through graduation with him," Marion recalled. "So, I accepted a two-year associate degree in business and went through the commencement with him."

How difficult of a sale was that to Marion? Keep in mind Terry sold his family on moving across Louisville a few years earlier, so when he convinced Marion to graduate with him, she knew he had a plan and she wanted to be a part of it.

But first things first. A few weeks after graduation on May 9, 1959, Marion Cecil became Mrs. Terry Forcht. Terry's friend, Bill Davis, was his best man and Marion's two sisters, Beverly Ann and Linda Sue, stood up with her.

Terry, in his pitch to convince Marion she should get her two-year degree at U of L, had told her he was thinking about law school. Not just any law school, mind you, but the University of Miami law school…the one in Florida.

There was something about the Miami area of Florida that attracted Terry. When he made the trip after high school graduation, it had not been his first exposure to the Sunshine State.

In 1945, Evelyn, her mother, seven-year-old Terry, and four-year-old Janey boarded a Greyhound bus for Miami to visit relatives. Being wartime, the four had to wait at each stop along the way for soldiers to board first, causing them to miss several connections.

And then years later, Terry and Marion did the bus thing together. "In 1958, Marion and I rode a Greyhound bus there," Terry said. "Took us two days, saw lots of little towns, and I never wanted to do it again. By then my aunt and uncle had been there for several years. He sold office equipment for a national company. We stayed a few days and liked the warmth, coconuts and palm trees. I really thought Florida was a fascinating state, and at the time the Miami area looked like it might have a lot of potential for us. We actually thought that this might be someplace we might want to live in the future."

There were friends and family, in the beginning, who questioned how the newlyweds were going to make it financially. Terry and Marion had a plan. Remember the Avery Book Terry had kept up for years with weekly deposits from his multitude of jobs? Well, he now had over $5,000 put back. As for Marion, she also knew the value of a dollar and had saved as well. Combined, they were going to be okay.

At the time, Miami's law school was the second largest in the

South, and the entire city was experiencing an upswing of growth and vitality that had included the university.

The new Mr. and Mrs. Forcht loaded up their car and headed to the Sunshine State. Terry was 21, and Marion 20, and on the horizon was a future neither could imagine.

But first they had to drive thirty hours, and then locate an on-campus apartment. And in Forcht style, they both found jobs. Marion worked full-time at the university, while Terry worked part-time in the school's mailroom.

Most of Terry's time was spent studying. Law school was tough for him. By his own admission, he had never been a good speller and he struggled with essay-type curriculums. But he made it through.

On May 29, 1960, the Forcht's first child, Ted, was born. With Marion no longer working, the couple set out to re-evaluate their finances. They figured they had enough money to stay in Miami another year, and Terry, deciding law school could wait, switched to the university's Master of Business Administration program.

In May 1961, he received his MBA degree with a concentration on finance. That wasn't the only celebration Terry and Marion had. On October 17, 1961, daughter Brenda was born.

When they left Louisville for Miami they had been a couple, and now two years later they were a family of four.

They were headed home. Terry stayed focused on his education, but he was a little undecided about how he and Marion were going to pull it together financially.

Now back in Louisville, he accepted a job in a brokerage house doing research and putting together a company newsletter. Always trying to better his position in life, he soon went to work in a training program with the Louisville branch of the Federal Reserve.

With a salary of just under $100 a week, combined with down

payment money from Marion's parents, the Forchts bought a small house on Kenlock Drive in Rolling Hills subdivision. With a mortgage payment of $87 a month, plus utilities, food, clothing, and gas for the Volkswagen they were now driving, Marion's role as a full-time mother and wife included keeping an eye on the bank account.

Terry, working full-time during the day, had now enrolled at U of L's night law school. With everything he did he tried to be calculating in his decisions. He had already proved to himself that he was a risk taker. The move to Miami proved that. Now, he and Marion had bought a house, and with two small kids and a $100-a-week-job, that was a risk, wasn't it?

He thought about an uncle who owned an icehouse in Louisville but knew he didn't want to do that. Then there was his grandfather, who owned a meat packing business. Terry had heard the stories about how bullheaded he was and how he had finally been put out of business by the meat inspectors. That had been a lesson on listening to people and following rules. And there was another uncle. He had been a respected lawyer in Louisville, and when he died, he was buried in prestigious Cave Hill Cemetery.

Terry was not trying to be high-and-mighty about it, but he was trying to be sensible about any decision he made regarding his family's future. He had a big responsibility. Terry and Marion's decision of law school at night and the Federal Reserve during the day just might work.

Work and school, work and school ... nothing new to Terry Forcht. He couldn't remember when he wasn't doing it. In Terry's life, Saturday's would sometimes permit a stint away from studying, so he would go door-to-door recruiting new members for the recently opened John Knox Presbyterian Church in the Westport Road area of Louisville. He enjoyed doing things for his church.

On May 24, 1963, the Forcht family grew by two more, with the birth of twin girls, Laurie and Debbie. Now with four kids under three, there was no way Terry and Marion had calculated this in their future plans.

There were classes Terry took in high school and college that, at the time, he knew he would never have use for. But how many people in high school or college know with certainty what's around the next corner? He didn't begrudge those classes; he knew they were part of the playbook toward getting an education. And he was hell-bent on keeping his eye on the ball.

Terry's rise from humble beginnings is not lost on his past. Although he says he's not one to dwell on what happened yesterday, but more on the present and future, he may not realize how much of his conversation slips back to his old neighborhood in Louisville.

Back then part of Terry and Marion's resourcefulness was paying attention to how they spent their money. With a family of six to support, they accounted for every dollar. For sure they didn't shy away from bargains, and within what could be described as a meager budget, they found room to give to their church and put away some for their future.

The Forchts, like eighty percent of American households in the mid-60s, collected S & H Green Stamps and Top Value Stamps every time they visited a gas station or bought groceries. It was the American way and those stamps could be redeemed for small appliances, and sometimes, even cash.

Terry's mother, Evelyn, often wondered how he did what he did. Spelling and grammar had always been an academic weakness for him, and despite it, he became a very good student. He was smart enough to know he needed help, and for much of his written work that help would come from his mother and wife. Terry regards his MBA and law degrees as two of his top achievements.

Failure was never an option in school. Not wanting to face the risk of washing out, he committed himself to studying and it paid off.

If Terry ever felt lacking socially or academically, he set out to accomplish something just to prove he could, and when he finished law school he admitted, "I'm not sure what I was supposed to do other than say I'm a lawyer."

By 1964, Terry had completed his goal. Now with a college degree, an MBA and a law degree, and a family of six, he figured it was time to make some real money.

"My parents never told me about the kind of success available to anyone who has a plan and works at it," Terry offered. "They were happy with the small home they had with its mortgage, as well as their small income from dad's grocery. I really had no idea what entrepreneurship was. When I went to U of L and started studying business, particularly the financial history of the United States, I began to get a feel for some of the things that were out there, and how the country developed on a financial basis."

There were lots of law firms in Louisville that could be job possibilities, but Terry, as only he could do, had another path he wanted to explore, and it didn't necessarily mean hanging up a lawyer's shingle.

"I just didn't want to do it," he said. "So, I used my academic degrees I had earned to see what options were out there."

Terry found a job placement agency in Memphis, Tennessee, that looked promising. He filled out all the necessary paperwork and waited. Soon he heard back from two colleges, one in Oshkosh, Wisconsin, and the other in Williamsburg, Kentucky.

"We visited Oshkosh and then Williamsburg," Terry said. "College of the Cumberlands in Williamsburg seemed more appealing. We liked what we saw and there was an opportunity to go right in and start teaching. It was a chance to learn while I went."

On the surface, Oshkosh might have been a better fit for the Forchts than little Williamsburg. Terry had grown up in a big city and lived for a time in Miami, so Oshkosh, five times larger than Williamsburg, seemed like a more logical place to settle. And for sure there would be a better chance of finding a "Forcht" name in the phone book than there was in Whitley County, Kentucky.

Terry's Tips
for Entrepreneurs

"Get as much education as you can. It will pay off in the long run. If you go to college, finish in three years."

Chapter Four

Teaching at U. C.

ℰℭ

Collège of the Cumberlands, now called the University of the Cumberlands, was a small regional liberal arts school, founded as Williamsburg Institute in 1888. Its students came mainly from the mountains in eastern Kentucky.

"We arrived in Williamsburg in 1964 with very little money," Terry said. "We had four children and a dog — all in a VW Beetle. We were packed in there pretty tight, so there was no need for seat belts."

Terry was qualified to teach several classes at the college, and when he saw they had openings for instructors in accounting, economics, law, marketing and finance, it didn't surprise anyone who knew him that he signed up to teach them all. His first-year salary was $4,700. With no classroom experience, other than what he had as a student, he put long hours into class preparation with lesson plans and all.

"I learned a lot from the classes I taught," he said. "In fact, Marion said I was my best student."

As in Terry Forcht style, it didn't take him long to start looking for other ways to make money. They had rented a house in the Highland Park area of Williamsburg that first year, but now they had found an old historic home on Main Street next to the Williamsburg City School that was perfect for their family.

They had quickly made friends in the small town, especially with other faculty members and their families. For decades mountain people have been stereotyped as "not taking kindly to strangers," especially strangers with an unusual German name. No one will ever know, but if Terry had moved to Williamsburg for any job other than teaching at the college, he might not have been so readily accepted. That's not an indictment on the residents of Whitley County, but just the way it was in the '60s.

The Forcht family had made an impact on the small town in a big way. But they weren't through. Terry had become the acting head of the college's Business Department, and he had invested in a couple of rental houses in town.

The young couple received a setback in 1967, when Marion was diagnosed with rheumatic fever. It was necessary to cut back her daily routine, and she spent most of her time in bed over the next several months. Fortunately, she fully recovered.

"Living in a small town was a blessing," Marion said. "Our next-door neighbor, R. L. Brown and his wife, Sandra, were so helpful and supportive. We also had other friends and neighbors who were there with encouragement."

Moving to Williamsburg was almost perfect for the Forcht family, except for one thing. The town didn't have a Presbyterian Church. They had been raised conservative Presbyterians in Louisville, and now they had a decision to make.

After much discussion, Terry and Marion decided the local Methodist Church had more in common with their beliefs than the others. There were, however, a few times that the Forchts were conflicted.

"At times the preacher liked to show film clips in the sanctuary," Marion recalled. "And we'd been told it was a sin to go to the movies on Sunday." Of course, Terry remembered his Sunday School teachers in the West End of Louisville telling him movies were bad anytime.

Being members at the Methodist Church in Williamsburg filled the strong, religious part of Terry and Marion's life, and it also gave them the opportunity to expand their network of friends. Living next door to the Brown's, it was only natural Terry met R. L. Brown's father, Lee Brown, an older, well-established lawyer in town.

Before long, Lee Brown was encouraging Terry to think about opening a law office in Williamsburg. He thought about it. In fact, he thought about it a lot. This, however, would be another risk, and one he was not sure he was ready to take. Things were going pretty good at the college. He had some income from several investments, so why would he want to take a chance like this, especially with a wife and four small children? How would he make it with no clients to begin with? He had bills to pay and it was a little scary. He tried every way possible to talk himself out of opening a law office.

"Law school doesn't teach you how to get into court or out," he said. "I didn't know what to do." Terry knew the law, but still, there were certain things in taking on a case he was uncomfortable with.

"Don't worry about it," Lee Brown told him. "If you get something you don't understand, I'll help."

By no means was Terry ready to break with the College of the Cumberlands. With the school it had been a two-way street, in that they were counting on each other. Terry enjoyed teaching, and, deep down, he had always identified himself as an educator. The college thought highly of him, too. His education had allowed him to be versatile in teaching an assortment of classes that would probably have required the school to hire a few more professors.

No, for now, he would stay where he was ... at the college.

Terry's Tips
for Entrepreneurs

"Don't borrow money to go to college. Work your way through."

Chapter Five
Law Practice

ℰↃႶჽ

No sooner than Terry had decided to stay true to the "bird-in-the-hand" theory at the University of the Cumberlands, he began having second thoughts. Why was he now doubting himself? One of his biggest accomplishments in his life was his Juris Doctorate degree. Why not put it to use, perhaps with his own law practice? Sure, there were certain things required of being a lawyer in a courtroom in front of a judge that he had doubts about. However, he'd overcome lots of things in his life to be where he was.

Terry knew the income at the college was probably never going to be what he was hoping. Then again, he had developed an inner guide that kept reminding him not to be in such a hurry to be a success.

Terry, however, was smart enough to know an opportunity when he saw one. How could he ever forget ole Buffalo back at Sandy's Food Market, seizing the opportunity when it was there? Why couldn't he have the best of both worlds?

He reasoned that he could still teach full-time and practice law part-time, just to make sure. And Lee Brown said he would be there to help.

"There's a space across the hall from me that's empty," Lee told Terry. "Why don't you go rent it? You can afford this one, it's only ten dollars a month."

When it was all done, with a chair, bookcase, lamp and curtains,

Terry had a total investment of fifty dollars. His second-floor office in the White Building in downtown Williamsburg, was open for business.

Terry had the good sense to know that associating with Lee Brown was a winner. Had it not been for Lee, Terry told others, he would have never opened a law practice, at least not at that point in his life. Lawyers in small towns don't always have enough potential clients to specialize in one area. But, Terry's varied business and finance background earned him a quick reputation as someone who could do it all.

As his client list began to grow, much of the credit went to Lee across the hall. People would call or come by Lee's office with a problem he didn't want to take on, so he would advise them to see Terry. "You need to see Mr. Forcht across the hall," he told them. "He's a specialist in that."

"It was a good place to start," Terry said. "And Lee Brown was a good teacher."

Another attorney Terry encountered when he decided to open his first law office in Williamsburg was J. B. Johnson Jr.

"I met this young fellow named Terry Forcht," said Johnson. "At first I had a hard time pronouncing his name. He had opened a one-room law office in the same building, and we spent a lot of time talking when times were slow. And in those days, believe me, they were slow."

On some of those hot summer days in his second-floor office, Terry would be visited by something he knew little about. Peacocks from the nearby property of Dr. Clive Moss would land on his open, screen-less windowsill just to check things out. "Those peacocks could stir things up," Terry recalled. "They made a loud noise that could be heard all over town ... sounded like they were yelling 'help, help'. It made for an interesting story."

Johnson continued, "I felt sorry for him, he had one room and used a manual typewriter. It was bare bones. He was from Louisville and didn't know many people. It didn't take long for Terry, however, to meet the right people.

"He had no local connections at all," says Johnson. "But in no time he had met Joe Patrick and then Dr. Barton and his wife Nelda. It seemed like before I knew it he owned banks, nursing homes and newspapers, while I was living from client to client," laughed Johnson.

"I taught some at the college (Cumberlands)," says Johnson. "On occasion I would have Terry come to speak to my class about how to get ahead in the world. The hours he told them that he worked were staggering. I think it might have scared some in my class a little."

At one time Terry and J.B. discussed becoming law partners. "I told Terry if somebody calls me to play golf, I want to do it. If somebody calls me to go hunting, I may want to do that, too." So, I said to Terry, 'If I did that you wouldn't put up with it, would you?' He said no, he wouldn't. We never became partners, but we've always remained close friends."

As his law practice was gaining traction, Terry spent quite a bit of time back and forth between the courthouse and his office. The contract work he did required his full attention, and he knew there were no shortcuts putting together leasing contracts that mostly involved natural resources like gas, oil and timber.

Terry still had an aversion to lawyering in the courtroom. It was, however, something he knew he had to do.

"My first court appearance was a criminal case. The defendant was charged with carrying a concealed, deadly weapon," Terry laughed. "I was working with another lawyer, Junior Teague, who'd been appointed by the court. At one point, the arresting officer was testifying that he walked up to the defendant and saw a gun in his belt. 'Make a motion! Make a motion!' Junior said aloud to me. But I had no idea what to say," Terry said. "The point, of course, was that if the officer could see the weapon in his belt, it was not concealed."

"In another court case, a defendant's shoes had been taken by the prosecutor as evidence. Well, I couldn't let the man go to court barefoot, so I bought him a pair of shoes," Terry continued.

Terry was doing a lot of legal work for people who owned businesses in and around Williamsburg, including nearby Corbin. "I was learning about business from all of the contacts I was making," he said. "And I began to see how you could build a business over time."

Terry's personality fit in easily with the people of Whitley County. Williamsburg and Corbin, only seventeen miles apart, are located in the proximity of the mountains of eastern Kentucky, but most people do not consider them mountain towns. They have produced several generations of proud blue-collar workers who have provided a quality of life that put roofs over their heads, clothes on their backs, and food on their tables. These were the same goals and values Terry had witnessed from his family and neighbors as he grew up in the West End of Louisville.

Williamsburg, which promotes itself as the "Gateway to the Cumberlands," is the county seat of Whitley County, and has the college.

Corbin's history revolves around being a railroad town. In its day, trains from throughout the Midwest and South utilized the railroad's switching yards, engine house and blacksmith shops. And, of course, Corbin is where Kentucky Fried Chicken's Colonel Harland Sanders opened his first restaurant.

The city proper officially sits in two counties, Whitley and Knox, with a third county, Laurel taking in an extended part of the town. However, due to a quirky segment of state law, a Kentucky city is prohibited from being in three counties. As can be imagined, there were growing legal and contract disputes in southeast Kentucky, and as usual, Terry's timing was impeccable. He had all the legal work he could handle.

Opening his law office on a shoestring fit in with how Terry had lived his entire life up to this point — being able to account for and justify every dollar and making sure he was able to pay as he went. By now, everyone in Williamsburg, Kentucky, knew Terry Forcht, and they also knew he would be successful.

Terry's Tips
for Entrepreneurs

*"Get married early, have children,
and get to work."*

Chapter Six
Joe Patrick

ଽଠଓଌ

O ne day a man walked into Terry's law practice that would forever change his life.

Joe Patrick was a coal and timber man. He was well known for buying, selling and making money. And because he was making money, he was also paying taxes. And that's where Terry Forcht came in.

"I did a lot of tax work in my law practice back in the day. That's when I actually filled out the forms," Terry said. "There weren't many lawyers who understood that kind of work. Joe liked that I was holding his taxes down. After a while he asked me to go around with him to look at some property he was thinking about buying. We would ride all over eastern Kentucky looking at coal or timber properties to buy."

Patrick was twenty years older than Terry, but he took a liking to the young lawyer with a name that was more difficult to spell than pronounce.

"After a while Joe decided he didn't like paying me for the tax work I was doing for him," recalled Terry. "So instead of paying me, he offered me a partnership in what he was doing. With me being a 50-50 partner, Joe would no longer have to pay for my legal service. That was my contribution to our business."

"Joe was very generous. We were never in the operating end of the coal, timber or oil businesses. What we did was acquire the land for people who wanted to mine the coal, and then lease it to them.

And Joe always believed in paying off his debts real fast. We would pay off the loans, and then we would own the property."

Terry and Joe spent years together, buying property and either leasing it for coal, or selling off the timber. "We'd make our money on the resources, but we'd still own the land," said Terry. "Coal got us off to a very good start."

Terry admired the core values of Joe Patrick. There was nothing uppity about him. He had survived the Great Depression, and then graduated from Berea College ready to teach school. But, first he joined the Army Air Corps during WWII. After the war, he went home to Whitley County to teach for the next five years in a one-room schoolhouse.

In 1950, Patrick decided to strike out on his own. He mortgaged his home in order to buy a piece of property in Red Bird in Whitley County. The investment paid off. His family still owns the property that continues to operate three working oil wells.

Terry recognized from the first day he met Joe Patrick that he liked him. He liked his no-nonsense approach to business, and the fact that he had an education background both as a student and a teacher. The pair became best friends, and Joe became Terry's first official business partner.

Most people in and around Whitley County described Joe Patrick as "a character". Even though he had no geology or surveying background, he had a gift for reading the land. Some folks around the area said they thought Joe could literally smell out the coal, timber, gas, and oil, and the potential it had when he "studied" a piece of land.

When he was buying and selling, it sometimes required multiple contracts that had lots of difficult terms and small print. Deeds and title searches, well, that's what Terry brought to the partnership.

For nearly forty years Forcht and Patrick, a bit of an odd couple, had a trusting relationship. Every morning the two talked to each other, telling what they had going on that day. Because of this, their business ended up owning more than 12,000 acres across thirteen Kentucky counties.

Those phone calls were about business, but they were also about a genuine friendship and respect they had for each other. "Joe would call and just say, 'Are you in or are you out?'" remembered Terry. "He was inviting me on another trip into the countryside, and whenever possible I was in, because I enjoyed tramping through the ridges and hollows with him."

Terry continues: "He enjoyed the outdoors. He knew the trees, berries and foliage. He'd grown up on a farm and had an interest in nature. He was a trader, a wheeler-dealer, with a vision that had an astonishing range. He knew regional lumber mill operators and understood the impact that an increase in U.S. housing demand could have on the value of Southeast Kentucky property with mature white oak trees."

Terry and Joe avoided deals with conditions. They did not want to deal with anything that would allot them shares of income from a mining company's future that might not come to fruition.

Terry readily admits that a big part of his success was being in the right place at the right time. Some would call it luck. Some would call it recognizing opportunity.

The coal industry was beginning to experience an upswing as Terry and Joe roamed around southeast Kentucky looking at property, and like anyone that has a success story, they found out that the harder they worked, the luckier they got.

Then in May 1967, the six-day war between Israel, Egypt, and several other Arab countries, led to the closing of the Suez Canal. The result was an immediate spike in oil and coal prices. Southeastern Kentucky coal that had been selling for $4 to $5 a ton jumped to $40 to $50 a ton as utility companies across the United States scrambled to meet the energy demands. Terry and Joe's business was booming.

Terry and Joe hired Thomas Richards, who friends called Tom Cat, to work for them during the '70s and '80s. Richards was a forester by training, but his main role was as a consultant. He assisted in figuring out property lines and calculating coal values.

"They'd visit a prospective property, estimate a value of its coal resources, and decide whether to try to acquire it," said Richards. "Joe Patrick would negotiate with the seller on a purchase price, and with coal mining companies on the lease. They'd borrow the money to buy the property and have its coal mined out within six months. They'd collect the lease income, pay the property loan off, collect a profit, and have full ownership of the property."

The stories about the unique relationship between Terry and his business partner and good friend Joe Patrick were known throughout much of eastern Kentucky. As different as two people could be, they were smart enough to realize what skills one had, the other needed, and vice versa. It was a business union for the ages.

Joe's son, Donnie Patrick, recalls: "One story I remember about my Dad and Terry was when they bought some property in Smith Hollow in Knox County. They had owned the property for several years and had the coal mined. Neither Dad or Terry had been back to check on the property for over a year, so one Sunday Terry decided to take Marion over and show her the property. Terry found Smith Hollow, and they began to go down the road looking for the house to identify the property. They made several trips down the country road looking for the house with no luck. Finally, Marion saw what was left of a foundation of the house and, sure enough, someone had stolen the house!

Sadly, in 2005, Joe Patrick died. The timber, oil, and coal guru had opened Terry's eyes to a whole new life and a different way to make money. Before Joe passed away, he and Terry had split their land holdings and mineral leases, donating portions of them to the University of the Cumberlands, University of Campbellsville, and the University of Tennessee.

Terry's Tips
for Entrepreneurs

"When you're starting out, look for a partner who has skills and knowledge you don't have. Then at some point, buy them out."

Chapter Seven
Starting in Corbin

ℬℭ

By 1968, Terry had resigned his full-time teaching position at College of the Cumberlands to devote more time to his growing law practice. Still, out of devotion to the college, he taught night classes for two more years.

That same year Terry and Marion made another life-altering decision. They decided to build a house and move to Corbin. The decision wasn't easy. They had picked out a building lot that overlooked the town, and with almost four acres, the wooded area would give Terry and Marion a scenic view that included watching deer, raccoons and birds eat from the feeding stations they planned to set out. And, by sheer coincidence, their new next-door neighbors were R. L. and Sandra Brown, who had moved to Corbin from Williamsburg a couple of years earlier. Years later, Terry recalled that "the price sort of got away from us." "I had to take out a second mortgage," he said. "It was a lot of strain for a while."

It didn't take long for Terry's network of friends and business acquaintances to grow. Terry had become an associate with the Sutton and Martin law firm in Corbin. His teaching at the college had provided an income until he established his law practice, and now, that law practice income had given him the financial means to get his other business interests up and running.

For most of Terry's life there had been no lights, no cameras, but lots of action. With a low-profile lifestyle, but a hard-charging business attitude, he had begun to expand his commercial real estate holdings, and his reputation spread that he was a top-flight attorney who knew not only contract law, but tax law as well.

In 1969, he was contacted by the Virginia-based Red Ash Pocahontas Coal Company. The company wanted to go public with their stock and hired Terry away from Sutton and Martin to do much of their legal work that included titles and lease contracts. Terry agreed to go to work for Red Ash on one condition – that they would also hire Linda Loudermelt.

When Linda was fresh out of high school and looking for a job, Sutton & Martin law firm was searching for a legal secretary and gave her a chance. She ended up going with Terry to Red Ash.

After a couple of years, Terry left Red Ash Coal Company and returned to the practice of law with Herschel Sutton and Paul Braden – and, once again, he brought along Linda Loudermelt as legal secretary.

Linda passed away in 2001, but her thirty-two years with Terry left her own legacy. Terry said of the lady he referred to as "Diamond Lil" (because she loved to go to Las Vegas and adored diamonds), "she wouldn't let it go when she thought she was right, and I was headed in the wrong direction. There were plenty of times I needed that," he said. She was also known for saying, "would someone answer that damn phone" when too many rings went by on the office phone.

When Herschel Sutton passed away in 1975, Terry stepped up to the position of senior partner with Paul Braden and his brother. Paul Braden, politically, was at the other end of the spectrum from Terry. But that didn't prevent the two from being law partners and close personal friends.

"Paul and I never let politics get in the way of how we handled our practice," Terry said. "And when it came down to law, even I couldn't outwork Paul."

Terry left the Braden law partnership a few years later and went into a new law partnership with Allen Trimble.

Terry and Allen Trimble were law partners for ten years. "I was a personal injury lawyer in our firm, and I learned a lesson from him. I would tell him I'd settled a case and he was relentless in asking me if I had received the check," Trimble laughed. "I learned not to tell him a case was settled until after I got the check."

Trimble witnessed it firsthand when Terry began to make his mark in the business world.

"He always had a thing about getting into businesses that required a license, or that were regulated by the government," Trimble said. "Radio stations, nursing homes, insurance, and banks. He felt like there was less competition, because there was no ease of entry."

During this time, the Forcht & Trimble law firm continued to thrive because of its reputation. With as many as five lawyers, an office manager, and a number of legal assistants and clerks, the firm was hitting on all cylinders.

"When you work with Terry Forcht, it's 24/7, but it's always professional", said Trimble, who retired in 2018 after serving 31 years as Commonwealth Attorney in Whitley County. "In all of our years together we never had a cross word."

One day a future lawyer by the name of Howard Mann came to Corbin as a summer law clerk for the firm of Forcht & Trimble. He had been accustomed to hard work back in his hometown of Ashland, Kentucky, while working at Armco Steel during college, so what could possibly be any harder? Not law clerking in Corbin, for sure.

"Somehow I got the idea that I would try to be the first person in the office in the morning and the last to leave," says Mann. "The problem is that meant that I had to be there before Terry and not leave until he left. He arrived virtually every morning before

7 a.m., and rarely left before 7 p.m. in the evening. And he always worked on Saturdays, too. I lost a girlfriend over it."

Mann learned a quick lesson from Terry. "I might have learned more that summer than almost any summer I remember, especially about hard work and discipline," he added. "To this day I almost feel guilty if I'm not at my office on Saturday mornings."

All these years later Howard Mann is still somewhat astounded as to Terry's focus and the way he engaged the other nine or ten lawyers in his office.

"Even with all he had going on with his other businesses, he would routinely leave his office every few hours and go to each lawyer's office to talk about the details of what they were working on," Mann recalled. "He always found the time to talk about cases whether the matter was large or small. Details mattered to him, and he was always generous with his time and advice. And he always knew if you were working."

And even though Terry's law firm (by then named Forcht, Hoskins, and Sanders) was still his primary business focus, he was thinking about putting more of his energy and efforts into the other businesses he was involved in.

"There for a while, every attorney in Corbin had started out with us—lots of folks who later became circuit judges and prosecutors. It worked well, and it freed me up to spend more time with Joe Patrick, going around looking at land," said Terry.

By that time, Terry had Joe Patrick's partnership in timber and coal, he owned several office buildings, was a partner in five nursing homes, and had acquired three radio stations in Columbia and Hardinsburg, Kentucky, and Springfield, Tennessee. "I always found that it was good to have partners," he says. "They bring knowledge and experience that you don't have,"

"I left my law practice in 1982 because it became so limiting for me," Terry said. "It had very little connection to the business world, and it was no longer as lucrative as my other projects ... healthcare, gas, timber, and oil." A lot of his personal legal work was turned over to Corbin attorneys Wes and Jeff Tipton.

Wes Tipton recalls, "the first trial I had with Terry was a boundary line dispute for Hillcrest Nursing Home. The judge set the trial date for July 4th, expecting everyone to object because it was a holiday. Of course, every day is a work day for Terry, so no one objected, and the trial took place on July 4th. After it was over, Terry told me he learned two things – 'one, we need a new surveyor, and two, I found my lawyer'." Wes still handles the majority of Terry's personal legal work today.

Jackie Willis, like Linda Loudermelt, came to work for Terry right out of high school. Like many who work with Terry, they came up through the ranks, usually starting out at an entry-level position. But as they show their willingness to work and take on more responsibilities, their roles in the company expanded.

Willis began her long career working for Terry in 1982 as a part-time employee at Mountain Laurel Manor nursing home, a fifty-bed facility in Corbin. Soon she was working seven days a week.

After a few years, she was hired to work as an assistant to Linda Loudermelt in the Corbin corporate office. She learned well, and upon Linda's untimely death, became Corbin office manager. Her position with the company has become important enough that she is now included as a member of the Forcht Group Board of Directors.

"Terry wants things done right," says Willis. "He's a perfectionist. He likes to see if you ask questions. He also wants to see what you'll come up with on your own, to see if you know what's going on. If you do it right, he'll encourage you to do more."

Every Forcht Group employee has at least one Terry Forcht story, and although Willis has several, there's one she likes to pass along. "We were getting a new banking center in McCreary County ready for regulators to inspect the bank on a Monday morning, and there was still lots to be done. I was supposed to have left for vacation on Friday but was told I wasn't going until the bank was ready," she said. "All hands were on deck. That night, as everybody in the new bank building was working, I looked up and saw Terry come in the door wearing blue jeans. He got down on his hands and knees and helped scrub the tile. Then he helped set up furniture. The next morning the bank opened on time, ready for customers and regulators."

Jackie Willis is usually one of the first to see Terry each morning at his Corbin office, before he heads out to his Lexington office eighty-eight miles away. It's a drive he usually makes in a little more than an hour.

"He's usually here by five o'clock or five-thirty at the latest," she says. "You can count on it. He turns on all the lights and feeds the cat, and then he's gone. If I get to work and the lights aren't on, I know something is wrong somewhere."

The cat, Duchess II, (there was a Duchess I) makes the most of a laptop in Terry's Corbin office. "Terry doesn't use it, but the cat does," Willis laughs. "It keeps her warm in the winter when she sleeps on it."

Another key employee who started in the Corbin office was Roger Alsip. It didn't take Roger long to find out about Terry's structured work habits when he was hired in 1989. He was working as a CPA in Corbin, his hometown.

Three years out of college, he had never met Terry Forcht. But hearing that he was looking for an auditor at his newly acquired bank in Greensburg, Kentucky, he was interested.

"The first time I met him was when he interviewed me," Alsip recalled. "When I was hired I got on board pretty quick with Terry's discipline and work schedule. I had been used to long workdays, so it was not an issue."

Roger Alsip saw firsthand why Terry's structured work schedule was rapidly spreading among the company's employees from the top on down.

"Not only was it our employees, but the people in Greensburg who found out how Terry works," Alsip said. "We had a big snow there one day that closed many of the stores down, but not our bank. Terry put chains on his tires and drove two hours from Corbin to Greensburg to make sure we had our people there and were open for our customers. I found out early I wasn't going to outwork Terry Forcht."

That's one of many stories about Terry Forcht that have made him a legend in his own company.

"When I first started working for him, I had no idea of the breadth of his organization," continued Alsip. "And what's even more astounding is that the average person couldn't have picked him out of a lineup, because he is so low key."

Alsip is not alone when he says, "Terry's best skill is working with people. We get great leadership from him not only by his example, but from his knowledge. He never gets in a tizzy. He used to say to me, 'It's not as easy as it looks, Roger.' But I never thought it was easy."

Alsip's work ethic and ability to be a quick learner made him a big hit with Terry, and before long Alsip was taking on more responsibilities with the company. He eventually rose to Chief Financial Officer of the Forcht Group and a member of the Board of Directors.

Terry's Tips
for Entrepreneurs

*"Take time to build your business.
Don't get in too big a hurry.
It took me 40-plus years to
build my businesses."*

Chapter Eight
The Bartons

℘ℭ

I n the late '60s and early '70s, Terry came to know many of his business associates through political activities. He and Marion found that gatherings involving the Republican political party had become much of their social life. It was at one of these gatherings that they met Harold and Nelda Barton.

Harold "Doc" Barton, a local surgeon, was from an old established Whitley County family that had been a part of the Republican Party landscape for years. Barton was a delegate to the Republican National Convention from Kentucky in 1964, 1968, and 1972.

Barton had already established himself as a hard-charging surgeon, who seemed to worry about everyone's health but his own. Terry, on the other hand, had begun to ascend the ladder of success, both reputation-wise and financially. He had that inner drive, which somehow put him in position to maximize his structured work habits and tireless energy to succeed. Maybe he was born with it, or maybe it was learned. Regardless, those who met the young lawyer were impressed and gravitated toward him.

Even though he was ten years older than Terry, Doc Barton was impressed enough with Terry to hire him to do his estate planning and other legal work. Barton had been on the board of directors at Corbin Deposit Bank and Trust for several years, and he recommended Terry for a vacant seat in 1970. Not long after joining the board, Terry became the bank's general counsel.

Around the same time, the two men had become business partners in an apartment building that became the first multiple-family structure to be built in Corbin. Terry saw in Barton someone he could learn from, and who knew where their friendship could go?

"Anytime he was in the room, he could dominate the situation," Terry recalled. "He was very aggressive, but he was also very smart. People might have disagreed with Doc, but they always liked him because he was on such a high plane. It wasn't just chatter either. He always had a good point he wanted to make."

Doc and Terry were both adept at keeping up with the financial climate across the United States. They were well aware that President Lyndon Johnson had signed into law the Federal Medicare Program in the mid-'60s. The country was in a state of transition. People were living longer, work habits were changing, and with LBJ declaring a "War on Poverty," it would mean better healthcare for the aging population.

Doc Barton, because of some heart health issues, had stepped back from his surgery practice but had been paying close attention to the burgeoning new field of nursing home care.

One day in the early '70s Doc Barton approached Terry with another business opportunity. Terry listened intently as Barton discussed what he thought was the future of nursing homes in southeast Kentucky. Terry agreed with the vision and a new business partnership was formed.

It was decided that Terry's role would be his business oversight and management skills. He knew to make any nursing home financially viable, rooms had to be occupied, and that meant their facility had to be better than the others.

Barton put together an operational plan. It would be one that provided a standard of care better than anything in existence. It would feel more like home than an institution. The food would look and taste like home cooking, it would have certified nursing care, and yes, it would always be clean.

The decision to partner up and move forward with a new nursing home in Corbin was easy. It made good business sense on a lot of levels. However, the reality of making it happen was another matter.

Since nursing homes fell under federal and state government rules and regulations, the two partners had to work their way through the required red tape. A Certificate of Need was the first thing that had to be applied for at the state level. The Barton's long-standing prominence in Tri-county politics was an asset in getting the final approval for the nursing home.

Terry Forcht was now a partner in his first nursing home with Doc Barton and his two brothers, Bruce and Don (both doctors), Dr. Elmer Prewitt, and R. D. Pitman.

On September 4, 1973, Hillcrest Nursing Home opened for business as a 120-bed skilled nursing facility. Doc Barton was Hillcrest's first administrator.

Four years later, Barton suffered a fatal heart attack while on a hunting trip in Colorado. It was Barton who had exposed Terry to, first, commercial real estate, then banking, and finally nursing homes. However, Barton's death did not put an end to the Forcht-Barton business relationship.

Doc Barton's wife, Nelda, was never considered a wallflower socially or politically in and around Whitley County. Suddenly a widow at 48, with four school-age children, she decided to continue with what her husband and Terry had started.

Nelda and Dr. Barton had been married since 1951 and she was aware of his business ventures, especially the nursing homes. Politically connected herself, she was five times a delegate to the

National Republican Convention, a twenty-eight-year member of the Republican National Committee, and the first woman from Kentucky to address the RNC National Convention and call the meeting to order.

It became important to Nelda that she continue what Dr. Barton had started, and Terry encouraged her to stay on.

"I just felt like Harold had worked so long and hard, and this meant so much to him," said Nelda. "He always wanted to make sure the residents were treated with respect, got good medical treatment, nourishing food, and some fun along the way. I just couldn't let it go."

To make sure she was more than a name-only partner to Terry, she enrolled in night classes at the University of the Cumberlands, studying finance, banking, and business management.

As they began to acquire nursing homes, they quickly established a criteria for what they wanted them to be. They demanded the facilities to be of such quality that they would live in them themselves, or family members would also, should the need arise.

That time did come several years later when the mothers of Nelda, Doc Barton and Marion Forcht all lived in Hillcrest Nursing Home. Eventually Terry's mother, Evelyn, lived in the Corbin Nursing Home.

There were several similarities between Terry and Nelda. They were both staunch Republicans, both had parents who had been small grocers (Nelda's parents had operated a grocery store in Providence, KY), and both strongly believed in the importance of education. "I've always thought an education was the answer to almost everything," she said.

Suzie Barton Razmus, the daughter of Harold and Nelda, has some fond memories of the time Terry Forcht came into her family's life.

"I remember Terry coming into our lives and the excitement and hope when he was around," she said. "Because of a heart condition, my dad had been given five years to live. He was just waiting to die. When he met Terry and they went into business together, he seemed to find a new energy. He had found something to live for."

Suzie said Terry and her dad had the same vision when they decided to build a nursing home together. "There was nothing like it in our area at the time. It was a labor of love. My dad's personality had always been infectious, but bombastic, and I remember Terry being a calming influence in his life, even though he was quite a bit younger than dad." Bryan Barton, Doc and Nelda's son, who later was the Administrator at Williamsburg Nursing Home (the facility which was renamed for his father after his passing), said "Terry was the most motivated, goal-oriented person I'd ever seen."

"At that time mother wasn't in the work force," Suzie continued, "after Dad passed away, I remember the meetings mother and Terry had as they discussed the future. Ultimately she decided to move forward with the vision, stepping into Dad's shoes as Terry's business partner."

By 1981, Terry and Nelda co-owned five nursing homes and sixty-six rental apartments in Corbin.

After Nelda retired and became ill, Terry called her every Sunday afternoon. "It meant so much to her to hear all about the businesses," offered Suzie. "She would light up when Terry called. He was so thoughtful of her."Their friendship lasted through twenty-five years of business and another ten years after she retired.

Terry's partnership with the Bartons, first Harold, then Nelda, lasted for forty years. Nelda passed away in 2014.

Terry's Tips
for Entrepreneurs

"Don't borrow money unless you have to. If you do, pay on the debt every month until you pay it off."

Chapter Nine
Debbie Reynolds &
Nursing Home Group
‍ℰ⒟⒭

O nce Hillcrest Nursing Home was up and running for a few years, Terry and Dr. Barton decided they were ready to invest in another nursing home – this time in Hazard.

Terry would once again be crossing paths with someone who was destined for bigger things, and who would take on a major leadership position with what would eventually become the Forcht Group of Kentucky.

As Hazard Nursing Home began staffing up in 1976, a young nurse named Debbie Reynolds was hired. Debbie graduated from Eastern Kentucky University with a Bachelor of Science in Nursing (BSN) in the class of 1974. This was the very first graduating class of Eastern's new Baccalaureate Degree nursing program. One of the distinguishing characteristics of the program was the management courses required. These courses helped prepare Debbie for the important role she would play in Terry's future businesses. After graduation, Debbie worked at the Veteran's Administration Hospital in Lexington, KY and the June Buchanan Clinic in Hindman, KY, (Knott County). She was hired as the Skilled Unit Supervisor for Hazard Nursing Home two weeks before it opened. A week later, the Nursing Director resigned, and Reynolds was offered the job.

"I was hesitant to accept such a major responsibility," Reynolds recalled, "but I had met Dr. Barton through the interview process, and he asked me to come to Hillcrest to discuss the position with the Nursing Director and other staff members there." The staff at Hillcrest was very persuasive and Debbie agreed to accept the position.

As a lifelong resident of Knott County, Debbie's roots in Eastern Kentucky ran deep. One of her ancestors, Uncle Solomon Everidge, helped found the historic Hindman Settlement School. Her father, Archie, was a Southern Baptist minister who, together with his wife Evelee, founded the Montgomery Baptist Church. He also served Knott County as its County Court Clerk for a dozen years.

Debbie's insight regarding the people and health care system in Eastern Kentucky was invaluable as Terry eventually added nursing homes in Knott, Harlan, Leslie, and Wolfe Counties, along with homes in Corbin, Barbourville, and Williamsburg.

Debbie recalls the first time she met Terry. He and Dr. Barton made a routine visit to the Hazard facility shortly after she was hired. "Terry was very professional," she recalled. "and somewhat reserved, but he had a ready smile for each person he met in the facility."

"When Dr. Barton passed away, Terry stepped right in to keep the facilities on track. He kept in touch with Administrators of each facility with frequent phone calls and he visited the facilities on a regular basis. His input and advice were invaluable not only to his facilities, but to the long-term care industry in general," said Debbie.

In 1982, after several years as the Director of Nursing, Debbie was named Administrator of the Hazard Nursing Home. "I remember quite vividly going to Terry's office in Corbin to interview for the Administrator's position," Reynolds recalls. "I was concerned about all of the responsibilities involved with accepting the position, but one thing Terry said made all of the difference to me. 'I'm very confident you can do this job,' he told me, 'but I'm not sure you have that same confidence. If you can acquire the confidence, you'll be able to do the job."

"He was right, of course. Great leadership requires confidence, and I would add enthusiasm and optimism. Few people have all these characteristics, but Terry has them in abundance, and he has the ability to instill these qualities in other people. From the first day I accepted the position, his frequent phone calls reinforced these qualities, and helped me to learn good business practices. One of the things that Terry does best is to create leaders. Through daily phone calls and other communication, he teaches as he speaks. He also teaches by setting an example on a day-to-day basis. This ability has been a major contributing factor to the growth and stability of his companies."

Debbie relates that her early years as Administrator at Hazard Nursing Home were quite challenging but very rewarding. Like Hillcrest, several community leaders had been asked to participate in the ownership and direction of the facility. The original Board Members were Dr. Harold Barton, Terry Forcht, Dr. John Gilbert, Willie Dawahare, Dr. Cordell Williams, Leon Holon, Erman Wirtz, Ed Sigmon, Ed Clemons, and Dr. Elmer Ratcliff.

"Working with this Board was a great pleasure", Debbie recalls. "They were all well known in the community and were very supportive of the nursing home. We looked forward to the quarterly Board Meetings. Terry and Nelda were always present for the meetings which were most often held at the Hazard facility. An excellent meal prepared by the facility Food Service staff was always a highlight."

When Knott County Nursing Home was purchased in 1986, Terry asked Debbie to add "Corporate Consultant" to her job title. In that role, she assisted the Knott facility with transitioning into the new company. She trained the staff to do things "the Forcht Way" which remains imprinted deeply throughout the group, but especially in the nursing home operations.

A key component of "the Forcht Way" was consistency. "Terry envisioned growing the company quickly and believed, quite correctly, that this would be easier to accomplish if we standardized as many policies and procedures as possible from facility to facility," recalls Debbie.

In 1987, Terry asked Debbie to accept another new challenge. By this time, there were seven nursing homes in the Forcht-Barton group, which was then known as "Health Systems, Inc.". The story behind the acquisition of Wolfe County Nursing Home is one of the most heartwarming stories in the history and evolution of the Forcht Group.

Wolfe County Judge Executive Danny Brewer was contacted by Donnie and Vera Harris, whose nephews owned land on the outskirts of Campton, KY. Glenn and Leroy, "the Boys" as they were lovingly called, were mentally challenged and had been in a nursing home in Salyersville, KY for a few years. Their parents had both passed away, and their aunt and uncle were not able to care for them. The boys longed to be back home in Campton. It occurred to Donnie Harris that the land upon which their old homeplace stood would be a perfect place for a nursing home. Donnie and Vera wanted so badly to bring the boys home, they told Judge Brewer they wanted to donate the land for the purpose of building a nursing home. Judge Brewer started working on finding the right person or group to help them. He contacted Jim Maggard, a State Representative for Breathitt, Wolfe and Magoffin Counties, and asked him to help find someone interested in building a nursing home in Campton.

Debbie became aware of the situation when the Knott County Administrator at the time ran into Rep. Maggard under a "blue light special" at a Perry County retail store. He told her the story, which she passed along to Debbie. Debbie relayed the story to Terry, who was immediately interested. A meeting was arranged with Danny, Jim, and other local officials. At that time, it was very difficult to obtain a Certificate of Need to build nursing homes in Kentucky. The Kentucky Commission for Health Services Control had placed a moratorium on nursing home beds. Construction of new nursing home beds would not be approved unless a great need could be proven.

Debbie accepted the challenge of proving the need and was pleasantly surprised to find assistance from so many wonderful people in Wolfe County. Donnie and Vera themselves were well known, and their Pastor, Rev. Doyle Thomas and his wife Brenda, were as well. With their help, along with County officials and local physicians Dr. Paul Maddox and Dr. Ed Burnette, the dream began to look like it might become a reality.

On the day of the actual C.O.N. hearing, many Wolfe Countians descended on Frankfort. The Kentucky Commission was taken by surprise. The support and the testimonies were overwhelming, and many prayers were lifted up. The Certificate of Need was granted. Glenn and Leroy were coming home. They were the first two residents admitted to the facility.

Glenn and Leroy were soon joined by their cousin Frankie and his mother, and many other friends and neighbors, most of whom they had known all their life. The community made the Harris brothers "honorary deputies" and presented them with badges to help "Keep the Peace" in the facility.

Dr. Maddox became the Medical Director and visited the facility daily until the time of his retirement, when Dr. Burnette took over. Vera Harris became the Housekeeping Supervisor and eventually the Dietary Manager until her retirement. She is now a resident at the facility. The community still holds the facility in high regard and many citizens of Wolfe County beam with pride when speaking of their nursing facility.

Wolfe County Nursing Home opened in 1989, the same year that Hazard Nursing Home was named the Statewide Facility of the Year by the Kentucky Association of Health Care Facilities. This was a long-held dream of Debbie and Terry, the Hazard employees, Board of Directors, and volunteers. The new selection process was very meticulous requiring on-site visits and a great deal of documentation. It set a standard for the other facilities in the group to follow. Williamsburg Nursing Home also received the prestigious honor, not once but twice, in 2002 and again in 2013. Wolfe County Nursing Home followed suit, receiving the honor in 2015. The Forcht facilities have won many awards and accolades for excellent quality care, but the Facility of the Year Award was the gold standard for which all facilities aspired.

In 1998, Terry established Management Advisors, Inc. to monitor and advise all the health care facilities of First Corbin Long Term Care (previously known as Health Systems, Inc.). Debbie was named President of that group. In 2001, she was also named to Terry's First Corbin Financial Board of Directors.

Terry and Debbie have worked together for over four decades and neither is bashful about expressing an opinion. When they disagree, sparks can fly, but that is a benefit to the organization. Debbie's strong will and determination to get it right are some of the qualities Terry most admires.

Terry has his own Debbie Reynolds stories. "Debbie has a sense of character and is quite meticulous in the things she does. They used to tell me that when things were not done right, you could hear her high heels hitting the floor – click, click, click – on her way to have a little chat with you." Terry also recalls a number of years ago when the Hazard facility was having some union issues, and some of the staff had walked out on strike. "To make sure the residents were cared for, she stayed in the facility for forty-three days and nights. She eventually wore them (the union) out and they went away," he recalled. Two years later she was able to de-certify the same union in the Knott County Nursing Home.

In 2002, Debbie relocated to Lexington from Hazard to lead the new Lexington corporate office as Chief Operating Officer.

Her move to Lexington was somewhat bittersweet. Although she missed being involved with the daily activities of the nursing home group, Debbie welcomed the challenge of her new role. The "icing on the cake" was the fact that her two sons lived in Lexington. Her eldest, Dr. Gregory Aaron Reynolds is married to Kristie Dawn, and they have two children, Sophia Kaidyn and Lincoln Gregory. Dr. Reynolds is a gastroenterologist at Clark County Regional Hospital and Bourbon County Hospital. Debbie's youngest son, Kevin Elliot Reynolds is a music producer and owner of Broken Crow Studio in Lexington. He has two daughters, Lyric Grace and Piper Elliot. Debbie's husband, Gregory Reynolds, is a retired District Manager for the Social Security Administration.

In 2009, she was promoted to President of the Forcht Group of Kentucky. Although Debbie is no longer directly involved in the nursing homes (now called Health and Rehabilitation Centers), she is the one person, other than Terry, who Forcht company leaders consult for direction.

"I enjoy so much being involved in all of the Forcht businesses, but after several years away, I still miss the daily interaction with the residents and employees of our Health Care Group, and of course, I miss Eastern Kentucky", Reynolds states.

"I enjoyed a wonderful career in the health care industry and was fortunate to receive several statewide awards (Administrator of the Year, Corporate Employee of the Year and the prestigious Community Involvement Award named for Nelda Barton-Collings). None of these meant more to me than a special acknowledgement I received from the Knott County Nursing Home in my hometown".

In 2009, a state-of-the-art department for physical, occupational, and speech therapy opened at Knott County Nursing Home in the newly built "Debra K. Reynolds" wing. It serves as a fitting testament to a woman who is never afraid to speak her mind.

There are currently nine Health and Rehabilitation Centers in the Health Care Group. "I'm grateful to the many key employees who made my job so much easier throughout the years. Susan Arnold and Michelle Jarboe, long time regional Directors and Board Members in the Health Care Group, are two such persons," said Debbie. When asked about Debbie, Susan Arnold stated, "The one thing that Debbie insists on is that we always do what is best for the residents. Regardless of the situation and decisions to be made, she says 'If you don't know what to do, start by asking yourself 'what's best for the resident?' If you always do that, you will make the right decision."

It's an approach that has always worked.

A closer look at the evolution of what would become Forcht Group, reveals much of the credit for its rise goes to the early success of the nursing home business. It was here that its cash flow helped fund Terry's ventures into banking and other businesses. And since those nursing homes required a Certificate of Need from the state, there was little or no competition in the counties where the facilities were located.

*Terry receiving the Ira O. Wallace Award for
Leadership from the KAHCF in 2007.*

*The Forcht family in 2007, L-R: Ted, Brenda,
Terry, Marion, Debbie, and Laurie.*

Terry with brother-in-law Deac Heath and sister Janey at the Derby, 2013.

Ribbon cutting at First Financial Credit in Morehead in 2017.

Williamsburg HRC winning Facility of the Year in 2013.

Debbie's photo unveiling at Knott County Nursing Home, 2009.

*Granddaughter
Kristen Urbahn
with Marion Forcht
at Derby Day, 2018.*

Attending the 100th Anniversary of the Governor's Mansion in 2014.

Barbourville Health & Rehabilitation Center built in 2013.

Terry catching a fish in Big Sky, Montana in 2013.

2016 Derby Eve Gala in Frankfort. Pictured left to right: Eddie and Vicki Woodruff, Marion and Terry Forcht, Debbie and Greg Reynolds, and Donna and Roger Alsip.

The original Giant Fork in front of Forcht Bank, Lansdowne.

With Jack and Suzy Welch at the Club for Growth Conference in Palm Beach, Florida in 2015.

Attending the National Conference for Community Bankers in Palm Desert, California in 2016. Pictured left to right: Roger Alsip, Greg and Debbie Reynolds, Terry and Marion Forcht, Justin Badeau, Tucker Ballinger, and Eddie Woodruff.

*2012 NCAA Final Four in Dallas. L-R: Roger Alsip, Jackie Willis,
Tucker Ballinger,Greg & Debbie Reynolds, Terry & Marion Forcht,
and Eddie Woodruff.*

*Forcht School of Entrepreneurship
at the University of Louisville.*

*Taking the NetJet to New York City in 2013. L-R: Roger Alsip,
Tucker Ballinger, Tom Hourigan, Debbie Reynolds, Terry &
Marion Forcht, Eddie Woodruff, and Greg Reynolds.*

*University of Louisville School of Business Circle of Fame in 2012.
L-R: Tom Davidson, Stewart Cobb, James Patterson, Dan Ulmer,
Terry Forcht, and David Jones.*

In front of the Rockefeller Christmas Tree in New York City in 2018. Pictured left to right: Wayne Sanchez, Greg and Debbie Reynolds, Terry and Marion Forcht, and Eddie Woodruff.

Forcht Bank, Forcht Group Hamburg office in Lexington.

*$1 million donation to University of Kentucky
Gatton School of Business in 2014.*

Forcht Group Corbin Office.

Terry speaks to students at the 2014
Western Kentucky University
Radio Talent Institute.

Terry and Marion's grandsons, Craig, Eric, and John Shockley.

Terry and Marion's daughter and granddaughters,
L-R: Kendall, Debbie, Casey, and Kelly Warren.

Terry's 77th Birthday at the Castle in Lexington.

Forcht Group Annex in Lexington, Kentucky

Terry and Marion's grandsons at Derby 2018. L-R:
Spencer Beloin and guest, Stephen and Taylor Beloin,
Shawn and Courtney Beloin, Sam Beloin and guest.

Marion, Jennifer, and Ted Forcht at the Kentucky Derby, 2019.

Terry Forcht cuts the ribbon on the Hamburg lobby Grand Reveal in 2017.

Terry's bourbon barrel shaped 80th birthday cake.

Terry receives the Corbin Business Professional of the Year in 2019 with Mayor Suzie Razmus and City Manager Marlon Sams.

Terry's Tips
for Entrepreneurs

*"Be at least 15 minutes early for
every appointment. Respect the other
person's time, as well as your own."*

Chapter Ten
Radio Stations

ഇ)ⓒ

T he '80s were a busy time for Terry Forcht's business interests. He was opening or acquiring nursing homes, banks, and radio stations at the same time. People that knew Terry were amazed at how he could keep so many "balls in the air". But somehow he did it. Terry has often said, "I'm not smarter than anyone else, I just work harder." And while he did work harder, he was also smarter when it came to finding business opportunities.

Terry was serving as a director at The Bank of Columbia when he heard that Lindsey Wilson College was interested in selling their radio station WAIN AM/FM. He asked lots of questions and found out the station was the dominant one in the small town. It was somewhat of a risk in that this was an investment in an entity with no direct link to one of his existing businesses.

"With the right manager and salespeople, it was a business we could run from Corbin," he said. "We were able to take it on without extensive debt or personnel. Our only sure customer when we bought the station was The Bank of Columbia, but we believed we could make it go," Terry continued. After the purchase, Terry's son, Ted, was an announcer at the station for a short time.

Terry's media portfolio steadily increased with the addition of more radio stations. He focused on stations in small towns in Kentucky that had for the most part been underserved. "I believe there will always be a place for local radio stations. People in small towns want to hear the local news, high school sports, obits, etc.," said Terry. This small-town approach would serve Terry well in carrying out the blueprint to financial success in all his businesses.

"We believe in little clusters. If you have at least five or six of something, you can have centralized management, and that makes it possible to bring in more expertise than a single business would be able to do on its own. It's the economies of scale that make it work," said Terry.

Ed Henson of Henson Media in Louisville is a radio station broker who is a fan of Forcht Broadcasting. In the early '90s, Henson noticed that Terry was buying radio stations and wanted to meet him. He called and was invited to come to Corbin, where Terry met him at a local Jerry's Restaurant. "I was very taken by his operation," Henson says, especially how Terry was able to present a list of specific criteria for a radio station to be purchased. First, it must be the dominant station in the market and preferably the only station. Second, it should have good technical facilities with which to create and present programming, and a good power signal. Third, it must include its own real estate. Henson was wowed during his Corbin meeting. "I was very impressed. It attracted me to work with Terry." Henson has brokered deals with Terry multiple times, and he joined the board of Forcht Broadcasting in 2011.

Henson says he always learns a lot in meetings that include Terry or other Forcht officials. "They are always trying to learn, trying to figure out how to do things better," he says. "There is always a lot of intellectual curiosity. I put a lot of value on that."

Terry Forcht has a proven track record of putting the right people in the right spot, sometimes when they have little to no experience in what he's requesting of them. More often than not, Terry bases a hire or a promotion on work ethic. He has seen it time and again. If a person is willing to work and has some basic intelligence, he or she can learn the task.

One of those persons was Dennis Cupp. With no broadcasting background, he had worked several years in retail sales and managed a group of dental offices. He was perfect for the job of managing Terry's radio stations, because Terry knew about his strong work ethic. One of Dennis's first jobs was to upgrade the radio station facilities.

"We were behind the times, and only had one computer for our entire operation," Cupp recalled. "All of the properties we acquired had the real estate with it, but our facilities were not as good as they needed to be. We implemented a full-scale remodeling initiative the first year." Today, the Forcht Broadcasting radio facilities are unlike any others — all top notch.

Cupp remains on the board of the radio group, even though he eventually moved to a position in the Corbin corporate office.

Another example of Terry selecting the right person for the right job is Mike Tarter. Mike had spent nineteen years in the radio business in Somerset before joining Forcht Broadcasting in 2004 to take over for Dennis Cupp.

Admitting that he is "a broadcast lifer," Tarter understands and promotes the strong connection between the radio stations he oversees, and the small towns in which they are located.

"To attract and keep listeners, we have to keep them connected to what's going on in their town. Satellite radio or online streaming can offer music but cannot inform listeners about local school and road closings, and they don't broadcast local ballgames," said Tarter.

Forcht stations also do live broadcasts from local festivals, fairs, or other special community events. These are advantages the smaller stations have over larger stations, which cannot make the local connections.

Forcht Broadcasting currently has 25 stations in Kentucky, Illinois and Indiana, and Tarter visits them on a regular basis. And at least once a year, Terry goes with him. Terry believes there's no substitute for getting out of the office to see what's going on in his businesses. It's part of his hands-on style that has served him well.

Tarter likes to tell a Terry Forcht story that involved one of the stations:

"I was still trying to find my way around everything, when Terry called me one afternoon and said the station was off the air. I said, 'I'm on it Chief!' I checked, and everyone said the station was on. I kept asking, 'Are you sure?' A few minutes later Terry calls me back 'Mike, everything's okay with the station. The cat just crawled on top of the radio and turned it off.'"

Tarter also gives Terry credit for being his group of radio stations' first and only national correspondent. "During Donald Trump's inauguration in 2017, Terry did live on-air reports from Washington, D.C. to all of our stations," Tarter said. "And he was really good at it, very detailed. We had lots of listeners who said they heard him."

Terry's Tips
for Entrepreneurs

"Don't be afraid to take a calculated risk in business. You succeed, or you learn."

Chapter Eleven

Newspapers

ೕಾಂ

A fter purchasing several radio stations, Terry Forcht's second foray into the media sector was in 1983, when he partnered with Nelda Barton to purchase *The Whitley Republican*, a local weekly newspaper in Williamsburg.

"It seemed like something good to have," Terry said, looking back on it. "We had banks, real estate, and nursing homes in Williamsburg and Corbin that needed to advertise. I had no background in newspapers at the time, but Nelda and I, being in politics, felt it was something we needed to be involved in — a good way to spread the message."

Terry was always looking for the right opportunity, and the newspaper seemed to fit. However, for it to fit just right, he had to have the right person engaged who knew the business.

That person was Don Estep. Estep started his career in radio, having worked several University of Kentucky basketball games as a student while majoring in broadcast journalism. But equally important, he was a Corbin boy, well respected and considered the Corbin High School "Voice of the Redhounds" for many years.

Estep also had experience with the newspaper in nearby London, where he was the advertising manager for renowned Kentucky journalist Al Smith, who owned the paper. *The Times-Tribune*, a Corbin daily newspaper, was big competition for the *Whitley Republican*, so Estep knew if his paper was going to have a chance, it would have to up its game.

He found that Terry was open to changes, and Estep came up with a big one.

In 1987, the *Whitley Republican* was re-introduced as *Corbin This Week*.

"We were playing on what *USA Today* had done in 1982," said Estep. "Terry was open to all suggestions. We produced our paper with the new generation of computers that allowed for desktop publishing."

The colorful, new local paper was a success. Over the years there had been several attempts to publish a competing newspaper up against the *Times-Tribune*, but all had failed.

Terry and Estep were just getting started. In 1992, *Corbin This Week* changed its name to the *News-Journal*, and then, unbelievably, three years later its circulation surpassed its rival. This was big ... really big, because with this milestone came a certification as the official legal newspaper of Whitley County, meaning *The News-Journal* was the recipient of county government's legal advertising and notices of all official activities.

The newspaper, over the years, has been recognized with numerous Kentucky Press Association awards for excellence in its respective category, and today is the third largest circulation weekly newspaper in Kentucky.

It is a common tactic for newspaper owners across the country to impart their influence, especially in political matters, in their publications.

"Terry has always kept a hands-off approach to the editorial policy and news coverage of our newspaper," says Estep. "The newspaper does not actively promote Terry or his business enterprises. And, any of the Forcht Group businesses that advertise pay the going rate that others pay."

Looking back on it, Terry says, "The paper was a good thing to own. It is a source of influence, but not necessarily a source of big revenue."

A business failure by Terry Forcht is as shocking as an April snow, and Don Estep has the rare distinction of having been involved in one of Terry's few unsuccessful ventures.

Terry and Don's partnership had experienced so much success in launching *Corbin This Week*, it only seemed logical when Terry zeroed in on building a printing plant in London, Kentucky. Not only would it print the *News-Journal*, but also two other publications, *Laurel This Week* and the *Somerset-Pulaski News-Journal*.

They had set about to see if a printing operation of the magnitude he and Terry discussed would be viable. Once again, Terry was looking for economies of scale.

The Duke Publishing Company was named for the actor John "Duke" Wayne, whose no-nonsense screen persona had long been an inspiration to Terry. In the lobby of the Duke Publishing was a life-size picture of Wayne.

Eventually, the Laurel and Pulaski County publications closed, and without them the printing operation was unable to continue. Terry had his own take on failure. "You could have gone to Harvard, paid high tuition, and not learned as much as we did from a failure. In all our businesses, we succeed, or we learn from our mistakes."

Terry eventually leased the printing plant to Community Newspaper Holdings, Inc., an Alabama-based company of newspapers in twenty-two states.

The Hamburg Journal in Lexington is another newspaper owned by Terry since 2003. It's a monthly publication that covers the news and events in the Hamburg area of Lexington. Corbin native Rhonda Reeves is the current Editor & Publisher.

Terry's Tips
for Entrepreneurs

*"You have to out work the
competition if you want to succeed.
There's no substitute for hard work."*

Chapter Twelve
Insurance Agency

ℰᏩᏳ

I n 1983, the same year that Terry purchased his first newspaper, Marion, by her own admission began to look for her place in the business.

"I was searching for an identity," she says. "Our children were all grown. They were either out of college or getting close, and I knew none of them were coming back to Whitley County, or I didn't think so."

Terry's growing business entities all required insurance coverage, and there was an ever-expanding group of employees, as well as business associates not directly related to his companies, who potentially might need insurance, too.

It made perfectly good business sense for Key Insurance Agency in Williamsburg to begin operating with Marion Forcht at the helm. "We brought in Bill Survant, an insurance man in Lexington, to teach us how to run an agency," Marion recalled.

"I stayed in the office keeping the books, filling out the details on applications, and doing the necessary paperwork required," Marion said. "The very first policy we wrote was to Joe Patrick's son, Donnie. He wanted us to write his auto insurance, and we still have his business today. Our son, Ted, also worked at the agency for a time."

Gaining insurance from people and businesses other than what the Forchts owned was important, because Kentucky law requires at least fifty percent of an insurance agency's business must come from outside its own affiliated companies.

Marion Forcht reflects on those early days and how far the insurance company has evolved. "It's quite different today," she says. "In those days we rated policies by hand out of our big books. Today it is all computerized, and the agent has very little to say in how to rate someone. The current way is much more efficient, and companies can track rates much better, but it's not as satisfying to put a policy together as it once was." Key Insurance eventually became Forcht Insurance Agency and continues today.

In 2015, the Forcht Group acquired CVIM Insurance Agency in London and Somerset. CVIM is led by Allen Marcum and specializes in commercial insurance

Terry's Tips
for Entrepreneurs

"Be persistent, make good choices, and stay focused on your time. Time is money."

Chapter Thirteen
Banking

ℰᴑᴄℛ

Terry Forcht's interest in banking began when he worked at the Federal Reserve of St. Louis, Louisville Branch, while attending night law school at the University of Louisville. He had been actively involved with banking since 1970, when his friend and business partner, Doc Barton, nominated him to join the Board of Directors of Corbin Deposit Bank and Trust. He later became General Counsel to the Board.

In 1981, things got interesting, and not in a good way. C. H. Butcher, Jr. of Knoxville, Tennessee, bought controlling interest in the Corbin Deposit Bank from Bob Daniel, a Corbin merchant. Prior to Butcher's purchase of Corbin Deposit Bank, Chuck Rapier, after several years of banking mainly in Louisville, had returned to his hometown of Corbin to become the bank's Executive Vice President. He agreed to stay on after the Butchers changed the name to C & C Bank.

C. H. Butcher and his brother, Jacob "Jake" Butcher, were on the fast track to building a financial empire "come hell or high water." The Butchers were very prominent in the Tennessee business world and in politics and had created the impression that they had access to practically unlimited funds.

Jake Butcher's United American Bank and C. H. Butcher's C & C Bank built what remain Knoxville's two largest buildings in the late 1970s and early 1980s. Jake ran for Tennessee governor in 1974 and in 1978, when he won the Democratic Party nomination but lost the general election to Lamar Alexander. Jake Butcher also led a group of businessmen who succeeded in bringing the 1982 World's Fair to (nicknamed "Jake's Fair") to Knoxville. However, over the years their failure to comply with federal and state banking regulations led to the collapse of twelve banks.

When C & C Bank became part of the Butcher's financial troubles, local directors Terry Forcht, Chuck Rapier, Nelda Barton, Jerry Hollifield, Bill Onkst and Jack Cloyd came up with the capital to re-establish regulatory compliances, square the books, and put capital and reserve ratios back into conformity.

"We met day and night," offered Rapier, "and Terry was available any time trying to help the bank. We were working to save our reputations. I think Terry was driven by the fact that he had a good reputation in his law practice around the state, and then someone from out-of-state came in here and did that to us. It became very personal." Eventually, both Butcher brothers served time in prison for bank fraud.

Ultimately, the FDIC took over all the Butcher banks and offered them to the highest bidder. There soon became a bidding war for C & C Bank. Terry led a Corbin group to buy it. However, rival bidders from London, Kentucky purchased it, and in April 1983, changed the name back to Corbin Deposit Bank and Trust.

In spite of the Butcher fiasco, Terry had come to realize he liked the banking business because it is regulated by the government. National banks must have a bank charter from the O. C. C. (Office of the Comptroller of the Currency) to operate. He knew it was not easy to get a charter, so once again competitors were limited.

After C & C Bank was purchased by London investors, Terry and the other former C & C Bank directors didn't like the fact that Corbin no longer had a locally owned bank. So, they set out to start one.

In February 1984, when the application was made to the O. C. C. to charter Tri-County National Bank, the original investors were Terry Forcht, Nelda Barton, Chuck Rapier, Dr. Bruce Barton, Donald Ashley, Dennis Myer, Alan Steely, and Melvin Tate.

Through it all, Terry's reputation as a courteous, professional businessman remained intact.

"Even with our own bank, whenever Terry needed something he would always ask, 'Would you have the time?' or 'Can you please do this?' or 'I need to have a new loan, can you please look at this?'" says Chuck Rapier. "He knew that we had to go through the correct process, and it was never a demand. You never felt like he was making you do anything."

In the fall of 1985, the charter for the new bank was issued by the O. C. C. With the city of Corbin being geographically located in three counties, Whitley, Knox and Laurel, it was an easy choice to name the bank Tri-County National Bank.

The investors had put up $1.5 million, with $750,000 as the initial working capital and another $750,000 in reserve. Chuck Rapier was named President and Chief Operating Officer, with Nelda Barton serving as Chairman of the Board. In spite of being the largest shareholder, Terry was Secretary of the Board.

Corbin now had four banks, but only Tri-County National was locally owned. Its owners and directors knew Corbin and its financial needs, and with the personal and business contacts of the investors, and the respect and goodwill they had built over the years with the Corbin community, the bank began to attract customers.

"In the beginning, you do business with some of your friends, family and associates," Terry says. "They deposit their money with you and borrow for mortgages, new cars, and to open or expand a business. But there are limits, even for a family member, on how far they are willing to bend financially to do business with you, versus someone else who offers a better rate."

Terry was determined that Tri-County National wasn't going to be just another bank. It was going to do a few things differently.

To begin with, it offered no-charge checking accounts. And on top of that, they paid interest on those accounts. And then in typical Terry Forcht style, the bank made itself more convenient and available to its customers by opening earlier and closing later. The bank was also open on Saturday.

In 1986, Terry was contacted by Luke Keith, the owner of the local newspaper in London, to let him know that Deposit Bank & Trust in Greensburg was for sale. Terry acquired the bank and added Luke Keith to the Board of Directors. One day, Luke came to the Board meeting with a relatively small loan request. The Board quickly approved, and Luke said, "if I had known it was going to be this easy, I would have asked for more!"

The Deposit Bank & Trust President at the time, Joe Shuffett, recalls "Terry took a very 'hands on' roll in the bank. He wanted to make sure the customers were taken care of. I spoke to him every day at 6 a.m. for many years."

Throughout the '80s and '90s, Terry's bank holdings grew consistently throughout southern and central Kentucky. In 1998, Terry's "small town banking" formula took a slightly different turn — he opened a bank in his hometown of Louisville, PRP National Bank. "Pleasure Ridge Park was a well-defined community in the larger Louisville market, so while it may have seemed to be a new direction for our bank group, it actually was true to our community banking focus," said Terry. In 2002, he followed that same course by opening First National Bank of Lexington in the Hamburg area.

Only one of Terry's bank acquisitions has been what is considered a "hostile takeover". That came in 2007 when Eagle Bank of Grant

County went on the market. By the time Terry found out the bank was for sale, the Board of Directors of Eagle Bank had signed a tentative agreement to sell the bank to another Kentucky bank — subject to shareholder approval. Terry decided he wanted to buy the bank and sent a letter directly to the shareholders (with an Open Letter to the Shareholders in the local newspaper) offering a higher price per share. After some contentious negotiations, Eagle Bank became part of Terry Forcht's bank holdings.

According to Cindy Young, Terry's long-time banking attorney with Wyatt, Tarrant & Combs, "To my knowledge, Terry's acquisition of Eagle Bank is the only successful hostile takeover of a bank that's ever happened in Kentucky."

Something you realize very quickly when you're around Terry Forcht — he doesn't like to lose.

"For many years you couldn't go across county lines with a bank branch, so if we wanted to start a branch in another county, we had to acquire a bank in that county, or apply for a separate charter," said Terry. "That's how we ended up with ten charters. The law was eventually changed, and in 2007 we combined all the bank charters into one charter and changed the name to Forcht Bank."

Today, Forcht Bank is the largest privately held national bank in Kentucky. The bank has twenty-six banking centers in thirteen counties in Kentucky and Ohio (with the 2018 acquisition of Cincinnati's Watch Hill Bank) and is led by President & CEO Tucker Ballinger. "Terry's entrepreneurial spirit filters throughout the bank, and his ability to connect to people at all levels sets him apart from most business leaders," said Tucker.

Terry's Tips
for Entrepreneurs

"Learn how to sell. Nothing happens until someone sells something."

Chapter Fourteen
Pharmacy

ℰℛ

When Terry and Dr. Barton first began acquiring nursing homes, Huff Drugs in Corbin and Hazard was the pharmaceutical source for the residents' prescriptions.

Dave and Pat Huff, who lived a few blocks away from the Forchts in Corbin, owned Huff Drugs. The Forcht and Huff friendship began when Dave Huff was a trustee at Cumberland College during Terry's teaching days. Soon it spilled over to a few business ventures together and then to becoming neighbors.

"We've been great friends for years, even though neither of our families spent much time socializing," Pat Huff said. "We were both busy with work and raising our children. As a business partner he is tops, always carrying more than his share of the load."

"We started Forcht Pharmacy because the law changed," Terry points out.

"There was a time in the nursing home business when you could not sell things to yourself. It was cost-reimbursed. The government paid compensation based on what price a provider charged. A company selling to itself could possibly have an incentive to artificially inflate costs."

But then the law changed, and everyone would pay the same price for prescriptions regardless of who owned the business. Medicare would pay a set price for medications, whether it came from a chain pharmacy or a private pharmacy, or even one the nursing home owns.

Nursing home residents were requiring tens of thousands of prescriptions in the nursing home facilities owned by Forcht, so in 1990, his company went into the institutional pharmacy business.

"We didn't waste much time," Terry said. "As quickly as we could get it organized we were in business." Once again, Terry knew he needed the right person to run the business. He didn't have to look far.

Larry Hill had been a fixture in the pharmacy business in Kentucky for a number of years. So, when he received a call exploring his interest in providing prescription services to Terry's nursing homes, he didn't need much time to make a decision and said, "Yes."

The Forcht Group pharmacy is classified as a "closed door pharmacy," which means it's not open to the general public. It is solely there to provide for the 1,100 residents in their nursing homes. Located in Corbin, the pharmacy, under the direction of Hill, is as up to date as any in Kentucky. Terry wouldn't have it any other way.

"From the beginning Terry has been very involved, making sure we understood the direction he wanted to go with the business, and then how to go about it," said Hill. "He has always provided us whatever we need to get the job done."

The pharmacy maintains modern computer hardware and the latest software systems to track the efficiency and accuracy in filling the prescriptions. With the exception of Sunday, daily deliveries are made from the Corbin facility.

Thousands of medical records and physician orders are maintained by the some twenty-five employees, which include five full-time pharmacists. And even though the public doesn't see the inside, in typical Terry Forcht style, its entry area looks like a hotel lobby. Beautiful crown molding, oriental rugs and comfortable chairs add to the charm of working there.

Hill likes to tell of the reactions drug company sales representatives have when they stop by the pharmacy. "Pharmacy reps and group purchasing agents from all over the country have been here at one time or another," he continues. "They tell us our facility is second to none."

It's just another Forcht Group hallmark, part of the winning formula Terry has not only created but maintained.

Terry's Tips
for Entrepreneurs

"Look for opportunities others might overlook. We built our businesses in small towns in Kentucky."

Chapter Fifteen
Construction

ℰ⃝ℛ

In the 1970s, Terry began building new nursing homes, banks, and apartment buildings with the help of contractor Arvil Mays. Terry had known Arvil since 1964 when he and Marion moved to Williamsburg. Arvil's construction company office was across the hallway from Terry's law office. One of Arvil's early projects was to build Terry and Marion's home in Corbin.

"In the late '70's, I decided to bring it in-house and start our own construction company. It would be something we could control," said Terry. It also was an early example of Terry's "baselining" way of doing business — one company on top of another.

In 1979, Terry hired Linda Loudermelt's nephew, Greg Johnson, as Construction Manager. Greg had just graduated from high school. "Terry kicked my b--- right in line. In addition to construction projects, I also took care of vehicles, going to the post office, painting, mowing grass, whatever was needed." And as Greg only half-jokingly remarked, "when a new construction project came up, Terry usually wanted it done in ninety days. Then if something went wrong, Terry would say 'don't jump out the window', which was his way of saying, calm down, we'll get it corrected."

As Terry's business acquisitions and startups continued, Greg and Arvil (who was still an independent contractor) could usually be found working together on job sites that included new nursing homes, building and renovating the Corbin corporate offices, or building new banks around the state. Greg was promoted to President of Forcht Construction in 2004, and Arvil Mays became a Forcht Construction full-time employee in 2005. Arvil retired in 2018.

In 2011, Forcht Construction began building the crown jewel of nursing homes in Barbourville. It opened to residents on Dec. 2, 2013. Today, the Barbourville Health and Rehabilitation Center, a $13 million, 135-bed facility, stands as an example of what health and rehabilitation centers can be. Forcht Construction also recently built the new "concierge banking" lobbies for Forcht Bank in Hamburg (Lexington) and St. Matthews (Louisville), and has begun to take on outside projects from other companies.

Terry's Tips
for Entrepreneurs

"Be prepared for setbacks. Take responsibility for your actions."

Chapter Sixteen

First Financial Credit

℘℃ℛ

As Terry's nursing homes and banks continued to grow during the late '80s and early '90s, another type of business joined the ever-expanding Forcht holdings. First Financial Credit opened in Corbin in 1992, offering consumers small personal loans from $300 to $3,000.

Several of the First Financial offices are located near a Forcht Bank, so that the bank can easily refer customers whose needs would be better served by a finance company.

"Banks and finance companies don't really compete against each other," said Terry. "Finance companies are limited on the dollar amount of loans and by law can charge a higher interest rate because of the greater risk. And it doesn't require as much capital to get started."

Tom Hourigan, a Washington County native, joined the Forcht Group in 2002 as an auditor. He quickly caught the eye of Terry Forcht and Debbie Reynolds, and a year later became the president of First Financial Credit.

"When we brought Tom in for an interview, we could tell he knew what the business was all about," said Reynolds. "He explained how the finance company business works. I was very impressed."

Once on board, Hourigan hired Charlene Powell, who soon became First Financial Credit's Vice President – Financial Services. Together, Tom and Charlene produced a company policy manual which helped to set the company on a new path for increased profitability.

In the meantime, Terry was interested in adding someone to the FFC board to work with management. Charlie Hall, retired President of Kentucky Finance, was hired to join First Financial Credit as a consultant.

"He taught me how to be president of the company," Hourigan said. "And what he said and did made an impression."

The company has experienced consistent growth, one small town at a time. "The key to a successful finance company office is to find the right local person to run it before you even open the doors," Hourigan continued. "We want to do business with customers we can trust because we have a relationship with them or strong knowledge of the community. Familiarity with the character of individuals, families, businesses, social ties and civic institutions are important to us."

Hourigan, like Terry, is an early riser, usually getting up at 4:30 a.m. every morning, except when he is in training for a marathon, then it's 3:30 a.m.. He is also a recipient of one of those daily early morning calls from Terry as he travels from Corbin to Lexington. "Terry's always telling me that there's no need to get in a hurry. Take your time and build it right. We're in it for the long haul."

Terry's Tips
for Entrepreneurs

*"Be proactive. If you make a
mistake, you can go back and fix it,
but don't wait, do what needs
to be done <u>now</u>."*

Chapter Seventeen
Insurance Companies

ಬಂತಃ

Terry Forcht's entry into the insurance company business was a somewhat lengthy process. In 1998, he purchased one half interest in Kentucky Home Life Insurance Company, with the other half being purchased by Farmers National Bank of Frankfort. Eventually Terry bought out Farmers National Bank's interest in Kentucky Home Life and became the sole owner. In 2007, Terry purchased Kentucky National Insurance Company from American European Group, who had voluntarily let the company go "dormant" after not writing new policies for several years.

As they say, "one man's misfortune is another man's opportunity." Since Terry was already in the life insurance business, he saw it as an opportunity to own a property and casualty insurance company. "It just seemed like a good fit for us," Terry said. Insurance industry veterans Enoch Roberts and Tommie Booth were tasked with getting the companies going again.

"It's a science and an art to know where to write policies, and we have confidence in the small-town approach. We try to select the right agents whose relationships will allow them to write good policies with good people. If we build a good base, the company will be profitable," added Terry.

Initial advertising for Kentucky National touted it as "the only property and casualty insurance company in Kentucky that is owned exclusively by Kentucky stockholders." Terry Forcht's approach to insurance was the same as his other business philosophy ... small towns.

In 2018, the Forcht Group added to its insurance holdings by acquiring Mountain Life Insurance Company of Alcoa, TN.

Today, Terry's son-in-law, Rodney Shockley, is president of Kentucky National Insurance, Kentucky Home Life Insurance and Mountain Life Insurance companies. He is also the Executive Vice President & General Counsel for the Forcht Group.

In 1992, Rodney Shockley was practicing law in Atlanta when he met Laurie Forcht, a real estate lawyer there. She told him her dad had some businesses back in Corbin, Kentucky, that involved banking and nursing homes.

"We were married the next year," Shockley said. "And Terry told me Laurie's only job was to make me happy."

As a visionary leader, Terry Forcht is always looking to the future. In 2001, Terry told Rodney he was looking for a family member to get involved in the business, and to someday be his successor.

"Over the next few years I got placed on several boards within the Forcht Group, and we started talking every Saturday morning," he continued. "He wanted me to get actively involved in all the businesses and become the general counsel for the Forcht Group." But Shockley wasn't sure he wanted to leave Atlanta, where he had grown up and gone to college and law school at the University of Georgia.

"I enjoyed being self-employed," he said. "But Terry can be very persuasive. I knew the time commitment it would take before I accepted the position, but our kids were getting older, so my time was more flexible." Rodney and Laurie moved from Atlanta to Lexington in 2008 and haven't looked back.

As one of the Forcht Group leaders, Rodney, like the others, knows daily when he and Terry will get on a phone call together.

For them, however, it is twice a day, 6:45 a.m., Monday through Saturday, and 5:45 p.m., Monday through Friday.

Terry's Tips
for Entrepreneurs

"Have an open door policy.
Keep everyone informed."

Chapter Eighteen
Forcht Group of Kentucky

℘℮

Prior to 2007, Terry Forcht's companies were collectively known as "First Corbin Financial Corporation." That unassuming name fit well with Terry. He had always been a low-key, behind the scenes type of entrepreneur.

But as his businesses continued to grow and employ more and more people, he felt confident that his business model would not only work in small towns, but in large cities as well. In 2002, the decision was made to open another corporate office in Lexington, while keeping the original corporate office in Corbin.

Once again, Terry turned to Debbie Reynolds to play a critical role in his companies. He asked her to move beyond her focus on health care and become the Chief Operating Officer of First Corbin Financial Corporation. One requirement of the promotion was that Debbie would need to move to Lexington from Hazard, where she had been serving as President of Management Advisors, Inc., the management services company for all of Terry's nursing facilities.

She agreed to take the promotion and moved to Lexington in 2002. One of her first assignments was to oversee the design and construction of the new Lexington bank building in Hamburg, and the opening of the new FCFC offices on the third floor of the bank.

A few years after opening the corporate office in Hamburg, Debbie convinced Terry that the time was right to put his name

on the companies and to take some credit for his achievements —
not in a bragging way, that would be against his nature — but just
to make people aware of what he had built over the years, and the
economic impact it was making statewide. Debbie also pointed
out to Terry that this rebranding would be good for business.

On November 10, 2007, First Corbin Financial Corporation
officially became Forcht Group of Kentucky.

Eddie Woodruff, a former advertising agency owner from
Henderson, Kentucky, was hired as Chief Marketing &
Communications Officer to work with Terry and Debbie on
rebranding the companies.

"The original theme for the rebranding — "Many Companies.
One Vision" — focused on Terry's vision to build the best
companies possible to serve small communities in Kentucky,"
said Woodruff.

An additional benefit of the rebranding was that it showed
that the Forcht Group was a major player in Kentucky business,
providing jobs for over 2,100 people in ninety-three separate
companies. "Our target market was business leaders around the
state," Woodruff continued. "Print ads ran in the Lane Report
and other statewide business publications, as well as ads on Forcht
radio stations throughout the state."

"The Forcht Group concept was more than just a new name,"
recalled Debbie. "We also set up a new corporate structure. A core
group of people was tasked with providing professional services
to all the 'profit-center' companies."

Today, the Forcht Group operates out of two corporate offices
– one in Lexington and one in Corbin. Forcht Group corporate
employees provide support services to all the companies in
human resources, marketing, information technology, payroll,
and accounting. The Forcht Group leaders are:

Terry Forcht – Chairman & CEO

Debbie Reynolds – President

Roger Alsip – Chief Financial Officer

Eddie Woodruff – Chief Marketing & Communications Officer

Leslie Jarvis – Corporate Human Resources Director

Greg Horsman – Chief Information Officer

Josh Marquis – Information Technology Director

Jackie Willis – Corbin Office Manager

David Witt – Assistant Corbin Office Manager & Healthcare Accountant

Greg Johnson – Forcht Construction

Tom Ulshafer – Creative Design Director & President of My Favorite Things

The Lexington Forcht Group "campus" has grown to include four buildings — Forcht Bank/Forcht Group, Forcht Group Annex, My Favorite Things / bank operations and training, and Kentucky National Insurance / Kentucky Home Life.

Terry's Tips
for Entrepreneurs

"The most important thing you can do is hire the right people to work with you."

Chapter Nineteen

The Right People

෨)෬

Terry Forcht readily admits that one of the key reasons for his success has been hiring the right person for the right job. It's one of the toughest tasks for any business, regardless of size. In fact, Forcht Group's employees are one of its biggest assets.

"To manage successfully, you have to find the right person," Terry says. "That person has to know the basics of the business and have the ability to identify what is important to monitor."

"They need to think similarly to us," adds Terry. "If they agree with us, we don't have to explain things as much. We can be confident in taking their opinion and in delegating to them. I always have key people around me. They are helpful and vital in making decisions."

For Terry, the decision-making process is extremely important. After he puts his key people in place, he always wants to know what they think about certain situations, and courses of action under consideration.

It might seem that Terry wants yes people around him, but he really doesn't. A person doesn't reach the level of success he has by associating only with those who agree with him.

"If I make a decision on my own without first hearing from our other people, I may not have the confidence in it that I should. I like to go around the room and ask, 'Would you do it? Why? Or if not, why not?' We try to come to a consensus. This usually results in a better decision."

Terry Forcht has thought a lot about making good decisions. Spending a couple of hours with him is like a semester of college. He asks questions, listens intently, and gives his take on things in concise words.

"If you try to make every decision and micromanage everything, you obviously will get to the end of what you do well," he adds. "With decision-making, we delegate as far down as we can."

But he always reverts to his basic instinct—work must come first.

"One of the first principles that you have to look at is to get the business first in your mind and get it going. If it fails, then everything else around you fails."

Working on Saturdays has become a Terry Forcht hallmark. It was something he figured gave him an edge. Terry's theory is that if a person hustles enough, he will then out hustle the competition. It harkens back to his lawyer days and the habit of working many hours to get the job done. It also conjured up memories of when as a young boy, he hustled pencils, chewing gum and night crawlers. He was doing something no one else was.

Terry does not hire key people who are not willing to work at least a half-day on Saturdays. And as he has proven, he doesn't ask an employee to do something he won't do or hasn't done. He works a full day on Saturday, and a half-day on Sunday after church. That's just who he is.

Terry's Tips
for Entrepreneurs

"If someone works for you and they're not getting the job done, let them go. Hire slow, fire fast."

Chapter Twenty

Spreads & Cycles

ᏽᎧᏨ

Terry Forcht has always been self-educated. Over the years he has learned about the importance of operating spreads in every type of business. For instance, in banking, an institution pays interest rates to depositors. Then it loans out that money at a rate that will allow for a decent spread, or as the bankers call it, "net interest margin". "I learned very early the cost that you pay for something versus the spread that you make," Terry says.

Perhaps it was something he was born with, but even in the early days selling pencils, chewing gum, and The West End News, Terry had a gift for business...good business.

As he began building his companies, he was in business for the long haul, not a quick buck. He would buy a company, hold it, and build on it. Flipping was not his thing.

"Selling means the end of that company," he said. "I want to hold it and build on it. Some people don't want to wait for the oak tree to mature in forty years. I just always had some talent for it."

His genius all along has been to keep an eye on the basic principals of business, and an almost unbelievable willingness to work harder than anyone else. And as only Terry can, he simplifies what makes him feel good about his business. "It's successful if we pay our way," he says. "If we make a dollar over our expenses, I'm happy."

His early experience in the coal business, both through his land deals with Joe Patrick, and his time as general counsel at Red Ash

Pocahontas Coal Company, showed him the impact and importance of cycles. Coal in eastern Kentucky has had many boom and bust cycles through the years. "I could understand how the pieces fit together. I could see the trends," Terry continued.

"A cycle can sweep people up and generate an excitement that takes many people's focus off the basics," Terry said. "It can be a positive or negative, too optimistic or overly pessimistic. It's difficult to tell when psychology creeps into a cycle and begins distorting supply and demand. This is what drives up prices and costs."

Terry Forcht has an uncanny ability to see cycles and trends others can't, or don't want to see. Forcht Group's Chief Marketing and Communication Officer, Eddie Woodruff, tells about how Terry, in 2007, told his group leaders that despite the current good financial times, they needed to start belt-tightening procedures and prepare for a deep recession.

He was spot on.

When the economic crisis that gripped the world's financial markets hit in October 2008, the Forcht Group was prepared. Their companies weathered the Great Recession, which had been the worst economic condition since the Great Depression of the 1930s, because they had cut overhead and reduced their exposure in advance.

"Too many people think whatever is going on now is going to last forever, whether it is a good time or bad time," he said. "The crucial question is, how long is this cycle going to last? I try to stay in touch with the general mood, the status of business cycles, and monitoring them is a priority. I read the Wall Street Journal, Louisville Courier Journal, Lexington Herald Leader, and several other business publications daily.

"With free enterprise, somebody is either going to take your business or you're going to take theirs," he says. "That's the way the system works. We do our best to be conscious of what's happening, anything that will give us a little edge."

It's an edge that can often be the difference between success and failure.

Terry's Tips
for Entrepreneurs

"Don't waste time going to sporting events when you could be working."

Chapter Twenty-One
Baselining

ഇൻൽ

Terry Forcht's business philosophy had always been, "Don't be in a big hurry, it will come." He had taken it slow and easy, and without much fanfare, he was building a business network that couldn't help but be noticed. He was using a simplistic business formula that might not have made sense to others, but he liked it, and that's what counted.

"Terry has a unique ability to foresee the business climate," Debbie Reynolds says. "And by using it, he's built his businesses one by one, building on each other. It's what Terry calls "baselining."

He has businesses that require insurance, so he starts an insurance company; he has nursing homes that use lots of prescriptions, so he starts his own pharmacy; he has to furnish his banks, nursing homes, and multiple offices, so he opens his own furniture store; his businesses advertise, so they buy advertising from his own newspapers and radio stations. In other words, all of the businesses he goes into individually have a purpose of helping the whole.

In the beginning, Terry Forcht may not have planned his "business-on-business" approach, but it didn't take him long to see that there could indeed be the means to an end by starting or acquiring a business that directly or indirectly connected to a business he already had.

Terry Forcht had his own ideas, visions, and ways to get there. Never has he gone into a business venture with eyes closed, except maybe that very first one with Joe Patrick. But that further shows

Terry's ability to read people. His inclination to rely on trust and loyalty in his business dealings was put to a test in the early days of his bank dealings with the Butcher brothers. He knew of them but didn't know them. Since then, he only deals with those he knows and trusts.

"I look for businesses that do not necessarily have to be run hands-on," Terry says in explaining his company's ongoing growth. "Of course, we need to go around and frequent them from time to time, but they are businesses we can track at the end of each month through financial reports."

"We don't have to work in the bank groups as much as we did in the beginning. We've got good people who run the banks in each market, so we don't have to be there all the time." said Terry.

Terry continues:"It is the same way with nursing homes. They're run independently. We have skilled people in the facilities to take care of the residents, but you, yourself, are not necessarily there. But we stay in touch with them, and of course, I still get daily or monthly financial reports from all the companies."

"Most things that we're in are charters, so we're not in overly competitive markets. The banks have charters … you can't just open a bank. And nursing homes have Certificates of Need, and all healthcare, pharmacy, and things like this you have to prove a need. Radio stations fall into that category, too. You have to have a license and frequency from the F. C. C," said Terry.

With the multiple companies Forcht Group owns, one of the businesses Terry has not become heavily involved in is retail. The one exception is My Favorite Things.

In 1998 Terry and Debbie Reynolds had partnered to purchase and develop a small gift store in Hazard, KY. That small store grew into My Favorite Things Furniture and Gifts which opened in the Hamburg area of Lexington in 2005.

"My Favorite Things is the only retail we're actively involved in, and a good portion of our sales are to other entities we own," says Terry. "Retail competition can be tough. It's something you have little control over. So, for the most part we avoid it."

The basics of good business practices, and keeping it as simple as possible, is what Terry says is another good reason for his success.

"Financial solvency is so important," he says. "We pay down our debts and are very conscious of how far we can go in expanding. We never want to bet the farm on one particular activity. So, we take it slow ... one block on top of the other. We aren't looking to double our size. We take on acquisitions in small doses. We buy businesses one at a time."

"I also like to keep the lines of communication fairly short," he says. "What we do, we do mostly here in Kentucky. There is a lot more activity in New York or Chicago, or London, but I think you improve your luck by staying where you ought to be. This is where you know what resources you have to deal with, and if any problems might arise, you can handle them fairly easily."

Terry has improved his lot in life. He has been asked time and again how he has done it, what his plan had been, what was his strategy to it all?

"There really was no master plan. But whatever we're doing seems to be working, so we'll just keep doing it," he answers. "I certainly think a little luck plays a role in success ... just being in the right spot at the right time. Still, I have never wanted to get beyond a base line, never wanted to bet the whole ship on one thing. I'd rather build block on top of block."

Although he keeps the same daily schedule he always has, Debbie Reynolds says Terry has, indeed, mellowed over the last few years.

"Over the last ten years he has traveled more," she offered. "He likes the Caribbean and frequently visited his son, Ted, in Marco Island, Florida."

Terry's vacations are usually of the three to four-day duration. They usually correspond with long holiday weekends such as Memorial Day, Labor Day, Thanksgiving or Christmas.

But even on these days away from his Kentucky offices, he's mentally still at the office. Getting up early, lots of reading and sticking to a full printed agenda for every vacation day keeps him focused.

"We often dread his return," laughs Reynolds. "We know he'll have lots of new ideas and materials for us to read. People often say that when it comes your time to die, you will never look back and wished you had worked more, well Terry is the exception to that rule."

Whenever Terry and his executive team travel outside of Kentucky on business, they fly in a "NetJet". Terry's fractional ownership (similar to a timeshare) in a corporate jet allows them to travel anywhere on short notice without the hassle of commercial flights.

"It is so much more practical for us to use this service rather than owning a jet outright," said Terry. "They prefer a two-day advance notice, but if needed, we can get a jet in eight to ten hours." NetJets, a Berkshire Hathaway company based in Columbus, Ohio, is the largest jet fleet in the world with nearly 700 aircraft in operation.

"A lot of mistakes in business are made because people are in a hurry to get rich. They want to start a company and do an IPO as quickly as possible so they can cash out." Terry says. "I don't think we've felt the urgency to get something done right now. It's more of a pacing; build what we can as long as we can. And then I have on my tombstone, 'I wish I could have worked one more day.'"

Terry's Tips
for Entrepreneurs

"Don't take money from outside investors. Work to generate the money you need to build your business."

Chapter Twenty-Two
Leadership

ℬↄↄↄ

T hroughout Terry Forcht's life he has been a good listener. It's a big part of what makes him a good leader and is well suited to his quiet, reserved persona. As he has climbed a sometimes disjointed ladder to success and riches, there have been many times when he needed to talk. And when Terry talks, people listen.

Great leaders often achieve their goals by listening and learning; and then it becomes their responsibility to pass on their knowledge to others. This is exactly what Terry has done in assembling almost a hundred businesses one block at a time.

Could someone follow his blueprint and achieve the same results? Probably not.

That's not saying others can't become successful, wealthy entrepreneurs. Many have and will. It's saying Terry's formula could perhaps only work for him. Knowing that no two fingerprints are alike, also means no two business styles are either. The franchise system has worked for some to a degree, but even then much of the success depends on the individual leadership at the grassroots.

Business startups aren't for the faint of heart, as statistics reveal that more than half of small businesses fail within the first four years. When Terry Forcht jumped in during the 1960s, while numbers on that sort of thing weren't in existence, it's a good bet failures were much more common.

In 2018, the state's economic development cabinet began helping to clear the landscape of obstacles and encourage entrepreneurs to think big, so Kentucky has become recognized as a place to ignite great ideas and grow strong companies.

"We need to keep working on the business climate in Kentucky, be more receptive to ideas that can keep people in our state," says Terry.

Even as that young boy on Olive Street in Louisville, he couldn't dream big enough to ever think of Forcht Group. What kid could? He, for sure didn't think of himself as a leader.

"I just caught fire at U of L," he says. Only the year before he wasn't even sure what college was all about. He knew however, he would be going there. His Mom said he would. "I went there scared," he said. "I thought, all of these smart people around, what chance do I have?"

What Terry didn't know was that all of those other freshmen students were just as uncomfortable and insecure as he was. What student doesn't remember those first classes in high school or college when called on by the instructor. Frightening times. Terry didn't know it, but he had a lot of others in the same boat with him.

"But, because I was scared, it caused me to become more focused," he said. "I knew I didn't want to fail, and it was then I realized I wanted to succeed." It was a defining moment in his life. With knowledge came confidence and with confidence came the ability to set goals and chart a course to achieve them.

"Whatever I did, I wanted to do a good job at it," he says. "I now had the degrees and education, and it was up to me."

Although Terry has always said he was never in a rush in his business ventures, for those around him that might seem to have been a misnomer. How could someone working more than twelve hours a day, six days a week not be in a rush?

Gene Hargis of Hargis & Associates, a long term care tax consultant who has worked with Terry for over thirty years, says,

"He's absolutely the most disciplined man I've ever known. I've been in the military, and he could hold his own against any military person as far as self-discipline."

Terry might appear to be a contradiction within himself. His personal work ethic is on fast-forward, while his structuring of his businesses evolves at a much slower pace.

Never accused of going with the crowd, it seems he has always known where he was going but figuring out how to get there required serious due diligence. True, his pace may not be as fast as others, but when he got there they knew he had arrived.

Terry has always been in control of his own destiny, never falling victim to the whims of others. He has always felt in charge of himself. If he wanted others to embrace something new, he asked them. He didn't tell them. It sometimes took time and effort with his leadership style, but it paid off.

It is human nature for some leaders to reject good ideas simply because they didn't think of it. In the business world there have always been employees who danced around trying to make the boss think they are the genius that comes up with anything good. This has never been a part of Terry's playbook. He not only collects ideas, he encourages them.

Much of Terry Forcht's success has been built around getting things done, and in doing so he has put his team in the lead early on. If anyone ever told him he couldn't do something, one of two things happened. Either he didn't hear it or paid no attention to it. For Terry it was routine … just another day at the office. Full speed ahead.

Terry is often asked the keys to personal success, not necessarily his, but success for anyone. Over the years he has told anyone who listens the same thing - "Save some money from every paycheck. Spend only for necessities. Don't splurge on something you don't need. Make a down payment in order to acquire something of value. And pay on your loans every month, even if it's a small amount."

Of course, there's more to it than that, but nevertheless these are basic rules Terry Forcht has followed to the T to help set his course in the business world.

He started early in collecting and inventing sayings that would serve him well in whatever business venture he was involved in. His friends, family and colleagues have affectionately referred to them as "Forchtisms." Some of them have been around even before Terry, and some have been picked up from books, tapes or old friends. If he liked them, he used them, because all of them are threads of wisdom, motivation and common sense. Here are a few Forchtisms and the stories behind them:

Start Right, End Right — Terry Forcht arises at 3:30 a.m. every day, seven days a week. He believes if you start the day right (meaning early) and end the day right (usually around 7:30 p.m.), and work hard in between, you will ultimately be successful. Terry Forcht's formula for success is very simple — outwork the competition. Put in the extra hours when your competitors are sleeping, playing golf, or watching a basketball game, and you'll gain a competitive advantage. It's this belief that's at the core of everything he does. None of the 2,100 employees at the Forcht Group put in more hours than Terry Forcht.

"People won't work any harder than they see you work, so you have to set the example," said Terry.

Let's Get In Over Our Heads And Work Our Way Out — Entrepreneurs take risks. Joe Patrick proved this when he mortgaged his home to get funds to finance his first land investment. Terry saw it firsthand, and the land that Patrick purchased then is still pumping oil today.

Terry has launched many businesses. "Don't be afraid to take a risk. Take it when you believe it's a good deal," he said. "Sure, it will be a work in progress, but bite off a chunk of something and throw all you've got at it; draw from all your resources. Then work your way out of it until you're in the black and successful."

Terry had always had strong support from people around him, believing in him and his ideas. Together they have worked out solutions, dealt with changes and challenges. Because of the inner strength of his company, Terry rarely gets rid of or sells a business. Instead his strategy has been to keep working until he works his way out.

Be The First To Arrive And The Last To Leave — This is perhaps the hallmark of Terry's "Forchtisms." It's what he has always been known for since those early days in Williamsburg. It might make for a long day, but for Terry it's just another day at the office. It's a rarity that anyone arrives at the office before he does, and he doesn't really expect them to. But what he does expect from his employees is when they do arrive, be ready to work.

It's also important to him that his companies dress the part. Looking like you mean business is an important part of his philosophy. When he was lawyering back in the '60s in Williamsburg, Terry owned a single black suit, and he wore the heck out of it. But it was his way of telling his clients, "I'm a professional, and I'll work as hard as I can for you."

This practice has never left him. Today his wardrobe has substantially expanded, and carried over to his employees, especially his group leaders, who daily wear a coat and tie for the men, and business attire for the women.

"In eastern Kentucky if you're wearing a suit they say you must be a preacher, FBI, or a banker," laughs Terry.

Change The Numbers Or Change The Faces — There's no hidden meaning on this Forchtism. Numbers are important to

Terry, and like any large organization, Forcht Group expects a lot from its key people. With some ninety-three companies, leader promotions don't always work out. That's why it may take several attempts to identify the right one.

That's also why Terry believes the financial statement is of utmost importance for understanding what is happening. Each month he reads the financial of every one of his businesses. However, it is his style to not wait for the month to end to get involved. That's why he insists that monthly financial reports be completed by the 10th of the following month.

"You can't spot trends if you wait," he says. "I read sales reports, occupancy reports, and other indicators well before the middle of the month. I ask questions. I ask what the "whisper number" is going to be. You know, ask my people to give me their best judgment of what they think the number will be at the end of the month."

With this approach it's easy to see how Terry keeps up with the staggering numbers he is presented. He doesn't wait for them to come in all at once.

"If you can learn to spot trends, to forecast the balance sheet, then, as we say in banking, you've run it through the proof machine," he adds.

Terry takes his numbers game a step further.

"By conducting our regularly scheduled board meetings at various locations, it gives me a chance to be on site, look and walk around, watch, listen, talk to people and ask questions."

This simplistic approach is just another way Terry can play his numbers game, realizing that if he doesn't know his numbers he doesn't know his business.

Big Hat, No Cattle — This old line is said to have originated in Texas, where big talkers had bigger mouths than spreads.

Terry is known for having a very accurate sixth sense. It didn't just happen over night, either. Decades of deal making have given him the ability of recognizing who has "cattle" or who merely wears a "big hat." He has seen it in land deals and banking.

"Be on the lookout for someone who makes a grand statement about their ability to finance a deal or follow through on a project," he warns. "But when it comes down to finalizing it, they don't have the ability to get it done.

"Sometimes when people are trying to get ahead, they will promise more than they can deliver. In the meantime, however, time and money have been wasted pursuing an impossible deal."

Terry has leaned on that sixth sense a lot in deciding if it is a good deal or whether someone has the capacity to meet a commitment.

Just Because We're Here — In business, sometimes just "being there" can set you up for time-consuming and troublesome situations. In a company as large and diversified as Forcht Group, it is routine and comes from all directions. And with some ninety-three companies to deal with, Terry easily recognizes why his businesses can assume a defensive mode when needed.

"Sometimes life is not fair ... It happens just because we're here," he says.

It's a line from one of Terry's favorite old war movies, Zulu, in which one of the outnumbered British soldiers under assault in every direction asked one of his superior officers why the Zulu are trying to kill them. "Just because we're here."

Sometimes You Have To Cull The Herd — Knowing when to "cull the herd" may not be a science, but instead more related to Terry's sixth sense.

Culling the herd can be attributed to livestock farmers who need to make sure what they have is productive. It has also spilled over into the business world as well. There are times when it makes sense to close down one of their business, because it was not profitable and no longer fit with the long-term vision.

Fire Fast, Hire Slow — Terry is a big believer in not rushing into a hire. For him due diligence is at the head of the list. Resume references are checked, credit reports are run, and criminal backgrounds are explored. It is Forcht Group's aim to bring the right person on board in the initial hiring process so as not to realize later a mistake has been made.

Terry's approach is to give the new hire the freedom and opportunity to accomplish the job he or she was hired to do. Most of the time it is successful. But when it's not, Terry is quick and decisive in making a change. This is the philosophy he learned from former General Electric CEO Jack Welch. "If you know, let them go," was how Welch explained replacing employees who weren't performing up to his expectations.

Everyone Needs A Number Two Person — Terry has always felt good leaders need someone who will give them honest and candid feedback. He knows this will lead him in making better decisions for the company. It may not always be what he wants to hear, but he knows, too, it is something for the good of the company.

The number two person, unequivocally, has to be trustworthy as well as a sounding board. Forcht Group President Debbie Reynolds says, "Terry trusts me because I will tell him the good, the bad, and the ugly."

Terry encourages these types of relationships among his staff and upper managers. Part of this philosophy includes Terry's insistence on an open-door policy. It didn't take long for an incident involving a door to become legendary within the Forcht Group. Despite subtle and not-so-subtle reminders from Terry to keep his door open, one manager repeatedly kept his door closed. Finally, Terry instructed his maintenance man to take the door off the hinges. Message received.

I'm Not Smarter Than Anyone Else, I Just Work Harder — No one works harder and longer hours than Terry. Never have, never will. But most people who know him would say he's also smarter. "Terry is immensely gifted for business," said Forcht Bank Chief Credit Officer Fran Fuson. "He's always looking ahead and saying, 'what can we do better?' and 'how can we grow?' His vision sets the tone and makes you want to drive harder to succeed".

We're Supremely Confident — This means Terry is very confident, without being arrogant, in his company's abilities to accomplish whatever the goal is.

Take Care of Yourself — Being able to work harder and to go to work at dawn requires good health. Terry, for years, has been tuned in to what it takes to carry on the rigid work schedule to which he adheres. That's why a proactive approach to maintaining good health is high on his priority list. It also carries over to wife Marion and several of his company's group leaders, who annually take executive physical exams at Mayo Clinic in Rochester, Minnesota.

"I try to eat sensible food like, bananas, Jell-O, cottage cheese or granola for breakfast," he says. "I walk my dog every morning fifteen to twenty minutes. I like to swim, too. But the important thing is we all have to keep moving and get enough sleep."

Although Terry doesn't take credit for coming up with all of these Forchtisms, he does in fact refer to them at the appropriate time and place.

Terry's Tips
for Entrepreneurs

"Stay active in church, community, politics, and tithe 10% to the church."

Chapter Twenty-Three

Republican

ℰℭ

M ake no mistake, Terry Forcht is all about the Republican Party. Always has been.

Terry's old neighborhood in the West End of Louisville, the best he could remember, was Republican. For his family it represented their values — less government, lower taxes, and high moral standards.

As Terry was growing his law practice in the late '60s, he became increasingly interested in politics and decided to run for state representative. "I ran against Elmer Patrick," Terry said. "He was a good guy and well-liked in the area. I lost."

Years later, Elmer Patrick had a story to tell about his campaign against Terry.

"Terry was and is a really nice person," said Patrick. "I knew I'd have to work hard to beat him. I worked seven days a week, going door-to-door. It was a Sunday afternoon when I pulled up in the driveway at this house. I saw a man sitting on the front porch, so I got out of the car and went up to talk to him. 'I'm running for state representative and would like your vote,' I told him. He jumped on my case. 'I can't believe you're out campaigning on Sunday,' he yelled at me. 'What's your name?' he asked. I stuttered around for a second, and said, 'Terry Forcht.'"

Dirty politics? Probably not. Terry and Elmer are still friends.

Even though he has never held public office, there is perhaps no one in all of Kentucky that is more identified with the Republican

Party today than Terry Forcht. It's no secret that he has been a major Republican donor over the years to local, state, and national candidates. But before he opens his wallet, he makes sure that his party's candidate meets his values — the values that were instilled in him at an early age.

Kentucky Governor Matt Bevin is well aware of Terry's loyalty to the Republican Party. "Terry Forcht is the very definition of professionalism. Above all else, he has never forgotten where he comes from, both literally and figuratively. In ways that are seen and in more ways that are not seen, Terry Forcht is a true servant leader. Kentucky is blessed by his vision and passion to serve others. I am grateful to know him as a mentor and a friend."

Terry's business reputation has been so far reaching that any Republican office holder wants him in their camp. Key Republican politicians can be seen shaking hands in Terry's Churchill Downs suite at the Kentucky Derby. This is not to say he doesn't have Democrat friends, because he does, including his former law partner Paul Braden in Corbin, and former Democratic kingpin Terry McBrayer.

Terry McBrayer is not your plain vanilla Democrat, just as Terry Forcht is not your everyday Republican. During his decades of politics, he has not only been a candidate for Governor, but a Democratic National Committee member from Kentucky, Chairman of the Kentucky Democratic Party, and a super delegate at the 2008 Democratic National Convention. At complete opposite ends of politics, the two have been drawn together because they genuinely like each other.

"Terry McBrayer has always been out there since I can remember," Terry said. "I've always known who he was." Like so many friendships, they start in a business relationship. The two Terrys began to share lunches together and before long the political wall began to crumble only to be replaced by a true friendship. It would perhaps seem unthinkable, but some of the Forcht grandsons have even worked in an intern program with Terry McBrayer's law firm.

"Some might wonder how, I, a liberal Democrat, and Terry Forcht, a conservative Republican, could be such close friends," McBrayer says. "Frankly, we are both personal and professional friends. A handshake means something to us. Our word is our bond. Why can't Congress and other government officials be that way? The country cries out for those types of relationships, so we can in turn move our country and state forward."

While both Terrys are lawyers, they share a work ethic that includes delivering papers in their youth, always working two or three jobs, and concentrating on business studies in college.

"Terry Forcht is a man of strong principles and values and asks nothing of others that he doesn't ask of himself," McBrayer adds. "He sets an example of those standards for his associates and colleagues. 'Don't do as I say, do as I do,' is his style. He is a good man in the old-fashioned definition of the term."

To substantiate just how close the two have become, a few years ago Forcht Group Chief Marketing Officer Eddie Woodruff called McBrayer to see if he would take part in a surprise 76th birthday party for Terry.

"I asked Terry if he had ever jumped out of a birthday cake," remembers Woodruff. "After a brief pause, McBrayer said, 'No, but I've got a feeling I'm about to.'"

It was a large plywood constructed cake on wheels, with a door large enough for McBrayer to squeeze himself through. Inside was a ladder leading to the top of the so-called cake.

The cake was rolled out, and at the appropriate time, Terry McBrayer popped out to the surprise of not only Terry Forcht, but the other two hundred people in attendance that day at the party.

Another long time Democratic friend is Glenn Leveridge. Glenn is a long time Kentucky banker who first met Terry when he came to work for Corbin Deposit Bank in 1974.

"I was twenty-six years old with a wife and three-month-old daughter," says Leveridge. "He had a way of making me feel really good about where I was in life. He was on our board and our best customer. There was just this presence about him."

"He's always been ahead of his time," Leveridge said about Terry. "He stays involved in the base of his businesses and doesn't take anything for granted.

I wanted my son to meet Terry, and as only Terry could say it, he told him 'you're a fine fella and let's stay in touch the rest of our lives'. What an impression he made on my son."

If anyone in Kentucky is a more devout Republican than Terry Forcht it might be Jim Host, a successful Lexington entrepreneur who started Host Communications.

Host has a long history of being on the edge of politics, but never being elected. He ran for Lieutenant Governor on the Republican ticket with Tom Emberton in 1971. It was then that he first met Terry.

"I met Terry when I was campaigning," recalled Host. "We've been friends since then, but it's only been over the last several years that we have become close friends." There are lots of similarities between the two, especially when it comes to getting to work early and going to bed early.

Terry likes to tell a story on Host. "A group of people were at Jim's house for dinner. Hours passed and his guests were lingering. It got close to Jim's bedtime and he told his guests, 'You don't have to go home, but you've got to leave here.'"

"Terry Forcht is one of the great Kentuckians of all time," Jim Host adds. "I think one of the keys to his success is his aw shucks, low-key approach to people. He's very deceiving in how he presents himself. It can disarm you."

Many business owners, especially ones who own banks, donate to both political parties to cover their bases and to make sure no customers are offended. Terry Forcht is not one of them. "No one wants to lose business over politics," he offers. "But, I'm proud to be Republican and what it stands for. I don't apologize for that. Being a Republican is good for business. It's the traditional pro-business party."

It says a lot about Terry. He doesn't pretend to play both sides, nor pass himself off as something he's not. If he loses business over his political stand, so be it.

Terry stays involved in small town politics as well. Former Corbin Mayor, Willard McBurney, had known of Terry for years. But it was not until 2006, when he filed for the city's top elected official, that he really got to know him.

"I received a phone call from Don Estep, the managing editor of The Corbin News-Journal," McBurney remembered. "He told me Terry and his staff would like to meet with me to discuss what I would like to achieve and how I would do it.

"Terry was very supportive of my ideas. I felt honored because I was aware of the huge investments he had made in several cities across Kentucky."

Terry's Tips
for Entrepreneurs

"Don't plan on retiring if you enjoy what you do. It doesn't say anything in the Bible about retiring."

*Terry and Marion
Forcht*

*2008 Forcht Group Board of Directors, seated L-R:
Roger Alsip, Ted Forcht, Debbie Reynolds. Standing: Mark Terry,
Terry Forcht, Rodney Shockley, and Dorsey Hall.*

Terry and Ted Forcht fishing at Marco Island, Florida.

*Terry at the corporate office
in Corbin.*

My Favorite Things furniture and gift store in Lexington.

Terry and Marion Forcht with Senator Rand Paul.

*A mural in the State Capitol funded by
Terry and Marion Forcht.*

*Dedication of the Capitol Rotunda plaque
with Governor Steve Beshear in 2012.*

Terry accepts the Reagan Award in 2011 from Rep. Andy Barr.

Fishing trip to Big Sky, Montana in 2013.

2013 Fundrasier for Sen. Mitch McConnell, L-R:
Terry & Marion Forcht, Elaine & Mitch McConnell,
and Cynthia & Hal Rogers.

2014 Centennial Gala at the Governor's Mansion in Frankfort.

Terry McBrayer pops out of Terry Forcht's birthday cake in 2014.

Covington Loan Production Office ribbon cutting, 2016.

Donald Trump Inaugural Ball in Washington, D.C.
L-R: Greg & Debbie Reynolds, Terry & Marion Forcht,
Laurie & Rodney Shockley, and Vicki & Eddie Woodruff.

Terry and Marion with President Donald Trump.

Governor Matt Bevin and Terry Forcht.

2017 Kentucky Derby.
L-R: Terry & Marion Forcht, Laurie & Rodney Shockley,
and Linda & Bob Davis.

$1 million donation to the University of the Cumberlands in 2018.

*Pictured with Vice President Mike Pence (center) in 2018,
L-R: Debbie Reynolds, Terry & Marion Forcht,
Laurie & Rodney Shockley, and Eddie Woodruff.*

2019 Bluegrass Hall of Fame photo with past inductees.

Ted and Terry Forcht at Derby Day, 2019.

St. Matthews Loan Production Office ribbon cutting in 2019.

Terry and Marion with Shaquille O'Neal, the Leadership Series Speaker, at the University of the Cumberlands in 2017.

Grace on the Hill Pastor Weyman McGuire,
Hal Rogers, and Terry Forcht.

Terry with U.S. Senator Mitch McConnell in 2016.

ILLINOIS

- Newton
- Olney
- West Salem

Forcht Group
OF KENTUCKY

K

COMPANY	CITY	LOCATIONS	COMPANY
★ CORPORATE OFFICES			● FINANCIAL SERVICES contin
Forcht Group of Kentucky	Corbin	1	First Financial Credit
Forcht Group of Kentucky	Lexington	1	First Financial Credit
			First Financial Credit
● BROADCASTING & PUBLICATIONS			First Financial Credit
WCKQ-FM, WTCO-AM	Campbellsville, KY	1	First Financial Credit
WAIN-AM/FM, WAIN-AM	Columbia, KY	1	First Financial Credit
WCDQ-FM, WIMC-FM, WCVL-AM/FM	Crawfordsville, IN	1	First Financial Credit
WGRK-FM	Greensburg, KY	1	First Financial Credit
WHOP-AM/FM, WHOP FM	Hopkinsville, KY	1	First Financial Credit
WWEL-FM, WANV-FM, WFTG-AM/FM	London, KY	1	First Financial Credit
WIKK-FM	Newton, IL	1	First Financial Credit
WSEI-FM, WVLN-AM/FM	Olney, IL	1	First Financial Credit
WSIP-FM, WSIP-AM, WKYH-AM/FM, WKLW-FM	Paintsville, KY	1	First Financial Credit
WYKY-FM, WTLO-AM/FM	Somerset, KY	1	First Financial Credit
WOWA-FM	West Salem, IL	1	First Financial Credit
WXKQ-FM, WTCW-AM/FM	Whitesburg, KY	1	First Financial Credit
Corbin News Journal	Corbin, KY	1	First Financial Credit
Hamburg Journal	Lexington, KY	1	First Financial Credit
			First Financial Credit
● INSURANCE			
Forcht Insurance Agency	Corbin	1	● Forcht Bank
Forcht Insurance Agency	Lexington	1	Forcht Bank
Kentucky National Insurance	Lexington	1	Forcht Bank
Kentucky Home Life Insurance	Lexington	1	Forcht Bank
Mountain Life Insurance	Lexington	1	Forcht Bank
			Forcht Bank
● FINANCIAL SERVICES			Forcht Bank
First Financial Credit	Bardstown	1	Forcht Bank
First Financial Credit	Campbellsville	1	Forcht Bank

CITY	LOCATIONS	COMPANY	CITY	LOCATIONS
		● **FINANCIAL SERVICES continued**		
ɔrbin	1	Forcht Bank	Lexington	3
anville	1	Forcht Bank	London	2
zabethtown	1	Forcht Bank	Louisville	3
ɪzard	1	Forcht Bank	Richmond	1
ɪdman	1	Forcht Bank	Somerset	2
ndon	1	Forcht Bank	Williamsburg	1
ɪuisa	1	Forcht Bank	Williamstown	1
anchester	1			
aysville	1			
ɔrehead	1	● **HEALTHCARE**		
ddlesboro	1	Barbourville Health & Rehabilitation Center	Barbourville, KY	1
eville	1	Corbin Health & Rehabilitation Center	Corbin, KY	1
estonsburg	1	Harlan Health & Rehabilitation Center	Harlan, KY	1
chmond	1	Hazard Health & Rehabilitation Center	Hazard, KY	1
ssell Springs	1	Hillcrest Health & Rehabilitation Center	Corbin, KY	1
merset	1	Hyden Health & Rehabilitation Center	Hyden, KY	1
nitley City	1	Knott Co. Health & Rehabilitation Center	Hindman, KY	1
lliamsburg	1	Williamsburg Health & Rehabilitation Center	Williamsburg, KY	1
		Wolfe Co. Health & Rehabilitation Center	Campton, KY	1
rbourville	1			
rlington	1	Forcht Pharmacy	Corbin, KY	1
ɪmpbellsville	2	Management Advisors	Hazard, KY	1
ncinnati	2			
ɔrbin	2			
ɔvington	1	● **RETAIL**		
ittenden	1	My Favorite Things	Lexington	1
y Ridge	1			
eensburg	2			

2020 Forcht Group Board of Directors

Seated, L-R:
Forcht Group President Debbie Reynolds
Forcht Group Chairman Terry Forcht
Forcht Group Exec. VP & General Counsel Rodney Shockley

Standing, L-R:
Forcht Group Chief Marketing & Communications Officer Eddie Woodruff
First Financial Credit President Tom Hourigan
Forcht Group Corbin Manager Jackie Willis
Forcht Group CFO Roger Alsip

✦

Chapter Twenty-Four

Giving Back

℘☊

W hen friends describe Terry Forcht, among the first words that rise to the top of the list is generosity.

His position in life has now permitted him to make a difference in many peoples lives in Kentucky. Since 2008, Forcht Bank, Forcht Bancorp, Forcht Group, or Terry and Marion Forcht personally donated more than $12 million to elementary schools, middle schools, high schools and universities in Kentucky toward their educational initiatives.

In 2007, Terry and Marion committed $4.5 million dollars to build the children's wing at Grace on the Hill Methodist Church in Corbin.

"One of my fundamental beliefs is that you should support your local church through tithing and giving of your time and talents," Terry said. "It came up in discussions in 2007 that the church needed more room for children's ministries, and since we had our own construction company, we decided to take on a new children's wing as a project, and we were happy to do it."

Kentucky Governor Matt Bevin commented, "His spiritual faith is the backbone of his decision-making process and it shows. His values are chiseled from a bedrock of integrity and are unmovable. This is increasingly rare in the world of business and is why Terry is so successful at all that he pursues," the Governor continued. "As rare as it is to cross paths with a man as gifted as Terry Forcht, it is even more unusual for such a man to be as generous and considerate of others."

Another substantial contribution from the Forchts came in 2009, when they donated $3 million to the University of Louisville to fund the "Forcht Center for Entrepreneurship."

"As former alumni, Marion and I were very proud to be able to give back to the University. Our gift and support of this fine program has enabled U of L to expand student exposure to more entrepreneurial challenges and opportunities," said Terry.

That same year, they gave $1 million to fund the Forcht Medical Wing of the Science Building at the University of the Cumberlands.

"We are proud to be a small part of the great things happening at the University of the Cumberlands and the excellent programs they offer to their students," says Terry. "It was here that we began to lay the foundation for what we have achieved."

The gift to the University of the Cumberlands wasn't their first. In 2006, the Forchts agreed to take the lead in the school's initial Leadership Speaker Series that has annually brought in a list of Who's Who speakers to the Williamsburg college. As of 2018, their gift has totaled $650,000.

The speakers who have taken part are: 2006, Roy Moore; 2007, Zell Miller; 2008, Stephen Covey; 2009, Ben Stein; 2010, Karl Rove; 2011, Mike Huckabee; 2012, Rudy Giuliani; 2013, Charles Krauthammer; 2014, Ben Carson; 2015, Fred Thompson; 2016, Will Graham; 2017, Shaquille O'Neal; 2018, Terry Bradshaw; and in 2019, Laila Ali.

Terry never forgot what teaching at Cumberland College had meant in his business success. And even though the college lays claim to two former Kentucky governors and five college presidents, no one has made more of an impact on the 7,000-student school than Terry and Marion Forcht.

"They have invested in the future of every student who steps on our campus whether they hail from Kentucky or from throughout the world," says Dr. Larry Cockrum, President of the University of the Cumberlands. "It's an honor to count Terry and Marion among the supporters of this University. Without their commitment and leadership, innumerable young students may not find the opportunity that exists for them here at the University."

His history of supporting higher education continued in 2014 when Terry gave $1 million to the capital campaign for the Gatton School of Business at the University of Kentucky.

"We recognized that the Gatton School was doing a good job of educating future entrepreneurs and business leaders in Kentucky," said Terry. "So, when they approached us to help fund the renovation and expansion of their building, we decided to make a $1 million gift. We had given a major gift to the University of Louisville in 2009, and we wanted to show our support for the University of Kentucky as well. Education is the key to moving our state forward and we want to support it in every way we can."

In early December 2018, the University of the Cumberlands once again was a recipient of the Forcht's generosity with a $1 million gift to help establish the Terry and Marion Forcht School of Nursing.

There have been many more gifts: $300,000 to fund the completion of the Capitol Rotunda Murals in Frankfort on the 100th Anniversary of the State Capitol in 2010; $175,000 to the general fund of the Kentucky Center for the Performing Arts over several years; $90,000 to the scholarship fund at Alice Lloyd College; $80,000 to the general fund of Hindman Settlement School; and $50,000 to the scholarship fund at Georgetown College.

For Terry, giving back also means giving of his time. Corbin neighbor Pat Huff tells about one of Terry's many acts of kindness. "Our newspaper delivery boy quit, so we had a difficult time getting a morning paper on a regular basis," Pat says. "Terry knew how much Dave (her husband) never wanted to be without his morning paper. So, Terry began delivering our papers to our garage door on his morning walk regardless of the weather." "I tell everyone that we had the world's richest paper boy," laughed Dave Huff.

Bruce Carpenter has been the Executive Director of the Corbin Economic Development and Southern Kentucky Chamber of Commerce for over thirteen years. As a lifelong resident of Corbin, he has seen firsthand the impact Terry Forcht has made on, not only his town, but also the entire region.

"I am appreciative of Terry's financial contributions to our city's schools, local volunteer fire departments, and non-profit organizations," says Carpenter."I think it's safe to say that Terry's investment and commitment to our area is something that will have an ongoing and beneficial influence for many years."

Terry's generosity and leadership has been acknowledged with several awards:

2004	City of Corbin Lifetime Achievement Award for Visionary Leadership
2005	Honorary Doctorate at the University of the Cumberlands
2005	Giving Spirit Award by the Kentucky Hemophilia Foundation
2006	Ira O. Wallace Award for Outstanding Leadership from the Kentucky Association of Health Care Facilities (KAHCF)
2008	Ralph Gabbard Distinguished Kentuckian Award by the Kentucky Broadcasters Association (KBA)
2011	Ronald Reagan Award from the Republican Party of Fayette County
2012	Boy Scouts Bluegrass Chapter Daniel Boone Visionary Award

2012 University of Louisville College of Business
Entrepreneurship Circle of Fame

2012 Kentucky Entrepreneur Hall of Fame

2012 Junior Achievement Bluegrass
Business Hall of Fame

2018 Excellence in Leadership Award from
the University of the Cumberlands

2019 City of Corbin Business Professional of the Year

Terry's Tips
for Entrepreneurs

"Read the Wall Street Journal, Barron's, and other business publications to keep up with current trends."

Conclusion

ഇറ

Terry and Marion still live in the same house in Corbin, conducting business as usual. And "as usual" for Terry, it's a blistering pace of multiple responsibilities that can become mind-boggling to someone who doesn't really understand his work ethic.

For Terry, it's nothing out of the ordinary. But, there is nothing ordinary about him. It was just the way he did it. It's just what happened along his path in life. Not necessarily the path he might have chosen in the beginning, nevertheless, when he went around the next curve of life, he was ready for another opportunity. He had the education, the desire, and the work ethic to get things done.

Whether it's a trip to the corner drugstore, travel to the beach, or climbing the ladder to a successful business, most want to get there as fast as possible. Not Terry. Perhaps in the beginning he didn't plan it that way. He was all about going someplace for sure.

But he has done it his way, in a disciplined, orderly style, fulfilling responsibilities efficiently and effectively. He has always presented himself in a calm, low-key, modest manner that is polite and, some would say, a little disarming. Beneath it all, however, has been an entrepreneurial streak that few could keep pace with, and even fewer could describe.

Could Terry Forcht have pulled off this incredible entrepreneurial success in another time period? If he started today as a college professor with a handful of degrees, what barriers would he face?

Would he meet someone like Joe Patrick, Doc Barton, or Debbie Reynolds? Maybe, maybe not.

The values embedded in him as a youngster growing up on Olive Street in Louisville never went away. Experiencing his initial taste of success, first in Williamsburg, then in nearby Corbin, proved to Terry that small-town life would be where he needed to put down roots.

Conducting his business, however, might be a different story. Sure, there would always be a corporate office in Corbin, but Lexington might be more conducive to overseeing the nearly one hundred businesses he now had, and at the same time growing the Forcht brand.

But the basis of the enormous wealth he has accumulated along his winding path, has been in small-town Kentucky. There were towns that for the most part had been underserved. He has seen their needs and met them. "I can't say I've ever had the feeling that I'm wealthy," he said. "But to a point I am content with the way things have evolved."

It's been said that if everything seems under control, you're not going fast enough. In typical Terry Forcht style, he has managed to prominently work even the car he drives into his world.

It's a 2018 Ford Police Interceptor that stands up to the rigors of being driven 60,000 to 80,000 miles a year. The white plain-wrapper is not your ordinary Ford blazing down I-75. Its appearance alone, with dual spotlights and an assortment of antennas, is not something anyone up to no good would want to encounter.

"That's why I like it," says Terry. "It lets me get back and forth to work hassle-free." That very well could be a description of Terry's driving style. But, too, it could be how his life has accelerated from a young boy on Olive Street in Louisville to becoming one of Kentucky's great entrepreneurs.

As Terry has assembled a Forcht Group leadership team he is comfortable with, he could be easing up on the gas pedal a bit. But, that doesn't mean his business engine isn't still humming.

He is still as active today as he ever was. "His stamina is incredible. He hasn't slowed down at all," said Corbin office Assistant Manager David Witt. Although much of what he once did has fallen to his group leaders, his daily presence at both the Corbin and Lexington offices is still critical to the success of his ever-expanding businesses.

The six-days-a-week calls to business associates and friends have become routine during those drives from his Corbin office to his Lexington office. And so have the daily 9:30 a.m. meetings with Debbie Reynolds, Roger Alsip and Eddie Woodruff. It's here that they do a quick review of the day's schedule, financial reports, donation requests, political events, and upcoming appointments.

Usually by mid-afternoon Terry is headed back down I-75 to his Corbin office, where he catches up with the day's going's-on until around 6:00 p.m.

On most Saturdays, Terry presides over a 9:30 a.m. off-site breakfast meeting at one of the Lexington hotels. Casual in appearance, but serious in discussion, it gives Forcht Group leaders an opportunity to hear what all the business groups are doing while reviewing the previous week and discussing what's ahead.

Most of the business group leaders are present, as well as corporate officers from accounting, marketing, human resources, and information technology. "It's good for cross-pollination of the business groups. They can learn from each other," said Terry.

Leading by example has been perhaps the single most important factor in not only bringing qualified leaders on board, but also keeping them. And in doing so he has developed a culture within his company that has inspired ordinary people to do extraordinary things. "How can I expect others to do something I wouldn't?" he asked.

Debbie Reynolds, the person who has worked with Terry the longest, says "If I were to describe the reason for Terry's success in one word, it would be 'tenacity'. His persistence and determination, even in the face of adversity, are characteristics which really set him apart. He never gives up. He keeps going until he has made every possible effort to achieve a goal. He definitely likes to win, and most often, he does."

The genius in Terry is that he recognizes the proper place for the past, present and future. His past has been a learning experience that has served him well. Business-wise he has experienced a journey that has allowed him to bring others with him through the mostly good times, while every now and then learning from a mistake or two.

Few people embrace the present as much as Terry. It's what he has worked for all his life. Today, right now, in the moment, is the fuel that keeps him energized. Every day that a person wakes up he or she must have a purpose. And Terry never loses sight of what he and those he has surrounded himself with have created. That is purpose enough.

He has assembled, one block at a time, a company built for the future. Back on Olive Street, selling newspapers, night crawlers, pencils, and chewing gum, he didn't have a clue what his future would be. As he attended college, however, he began to develop an inner drive to see what was out there.

He also gets a deep satisfaction in identifying and building long-term connections that have led to what is now Forcht Group. There were the Joe Patricks, the Harold and Nelda Bartons at first. Then came the Debbie Reynolds's, Chuck Rapier's, Linda Loudermelt's, Roger Alsip's, and Jackie Willis's. And, of course, there were Terry's early law partners.

Then there is his daily morning call list as he drives from Corbin to Lexington that includes Forcht Group President Debbie Reynolds;

Forcht Group CFO Roger Alsip; his son, Ted (who passed away in 2019); old friend Melvin Tate; brother-in-law Deac Heath; Corbin office manager Jackie Willis; Dennis Cupp and Brenda Hamblin in the Corbin office; First Financial President Tom Hourigan; Kentucky National Insurance Executive Vice President and General Counsel Rodney Shockley; David Witt, his Corbin office CPA, who often gives Terry a road report about construction spots and police locations; Tucker Ballinger, the president of Forcht Bank; Forcht Group CIO Greg Horsman; Forcht Group Chief Marketing & Communications Officer Eddie Woodruff; Properties Manager David Reese; Wayne Sanchez and Luke Groene in the Lexington corporate office; Forcht Broadcasting President Mike Tarter; wife Marion, as he makes his way into Lexington; and Owen Tackett, Forcht Group's head of security.

"It's the people you work with on a daily basis," says Terry. "And they grow on you."

No one book could possibly capture the full essence of Terry Forcht's life. These pages are a mere snapshot depicting a rare individual who has risen through the business world by doing it almost entirely in Kentucky.

Terry's days of growing up on Olive Street in Louisville instilled in him something that cannot be put on paper. The words just aren't there. He has managed to do it on his own terms, staying true to himself. And as he reflects on the foundation to his personal and business success, he credits several defining moments in his life.

"My undergraduate degree was what got me going," says Terry. "And then my MBA and law degrees were really important. I also think getting married and having children at an early age and having business partners with complementary skills really helped."

Terry, being a man of his word, and not being in a big hurry to finish the race, has been able to amass his large assortment of businesses one block at a time.

He likes to use one of his favorite sayings that he once heard from a land surveyor… start right, end right. Rising early every morning helps Terry start right. His tenacious ability to outwork the competition keeps him on target to end right. And though the end is nowhere in sight, one thing is for sure – the values he acquired in the West End of Louisville are the same values instilled in the Forcht Group today.

For Terry Forcht, it has never been about where he had been, but where he is going. Through the years, he has always stuck to his plan. It's not complicated. He's convinced anyone can do it and in their own way be successful – if they just keep working. As Terry likes to remind everyone, "nowhere in the Bible does it say anything about retiring."

Age has never been a roadblock. Quite the contrary. It's all in the way he has connected Forcht Group to his past, present and future. In 2019, he celebrated his 81st birthday– still going strong.

He often speaks to groups of high school and college students throughout Kentucky, and as might be expected, he is asked, "What is the key to your success?"

"It's simple" he says. "Three words – work, work, work!"

✦

Terry's Tips
for Entrepreneurs

*"Listen to other people's opinions.
This will give you a perspective you
might not have on your own."*

Epilogue

ಬಿಲ

So where is Forcht Group of Kentucky today?

Nine Health and Rehabilitation Centers throughout southeastern Kentucky now serve over 1,100 residents.

Forcht Bank is now the largest privately-held national bank in Kentucky, with twenty-six banking locations in thirteen counties in Kentucky (and one county in Ohio). Forcht Bank currently has over $1.2 billion in total assets with more than $125 million in capital. In 2018, Forcht Bank acquired Watch Hill Bank in Cincinnati, it's first entry into Ohio.

Forcht Broadcasting has 25 radio stations in nine markets in Kentucky, Indiana, and Illinois, making it the largest radio group based in Kentucky.

Kentucky National Insurance Company is represented by 150 independent insurance agents throughout Kentucky, and another fifty in Tennessee. It remains the only property and casualty insurance company in Kentucky owned by Kentucky shareholders.

Kentucky Home Life Insurance Company and Mountain Life Insurance Company offer life insurance products throughout Kentucky and Tennessee.

First Financial Credit has twenty offices throughout Kentucky.

Other Forcht entities include Key Technology, the Forcht Group's technology department; and real estate holdings that include apartments, office buildings, and shopping centers.

In total, today's Forcht Group includes some ninety-three businesses that employ over 2,100 people. There is nothing more noble in America than creating jobs. That's what entrepreneurs do. That's what Terry Forcht does.

✦

Terry's Tips
for Entrepreneurs

"Treat people with respect and they'll respect you in turn."

Timeline of Businesses
Date Started or Acquired, Original Name of Company

🙚🙙

Nursing Home Group

January 1972	Hillcrest Nursing Home	December 1985	Harlan Nursing Home
December 1974	Hazard Nursing Home	January 1986	Knott Co. Nursing Home
February 1976	Williamsburg Nursing Home	September 1988	Wolfe County Health Care Center
August 1979	Corbin Nursing Home	January 1990	Institutional Pharmacy
June 1981	Valley Park Convalescent Center	February 2005	Hyden Nursing Home

Bank Group

September 1985	Tri-County National Bank	September 1998	P.R.P. National Bank
December 1986	Deposit Bank & Trust	October 2002	First National Bank of Lexington
July 1989	Williamsburg National Bank	April 2001	Boone National Bank
December 1990	Campbellsville National Bank	November 2007	Eagle Bank
January 1996	Laurel National Bank	December 2007	Forcht Bank
August 1997	Somerset National Bank	June 2018	Watch Hill Bank

Radio Stations

July 1981	Key Broadcasting Inc	September 1986	C.V.L. Broadcasting Inc
December 1981	Tri-County Radio Broadcasting Inc	April 1987	V.L.N. Broadcasting Inc
		May 1992	F.T.G. Broadcasting Inc
March 1982	H.I.C. Broadcasting Inc	January 1993	I.A.I. Broadcasting Inc
November 1983	S.I.P. Broadcasting Inc	January 1994	P.R.S. Broadcasting Inc
August 1985	T.C.W. Broadcasting Inc	July 1999	H.O.P. Broadcasting Inc

First Financial Credit

October 1993	Corbin	April 2008	Richmond
August 1994	London	December 2009	Barbourville
December 1994	Whitley City	July 2010	Bardstown
March 1996	Middlesboro	October 2010	Williamsburg
August 1997	Somerset	February 2011	Danville
October 1999	Elizabethtown	June 2014	Louisa
May 2002	Hazard	July 2014	Campbellsville
December 2004	Pikeville	June 2015	Manchester
June 2005	Prestonsburg	April 2016	Hindman
October 2005	Maysville	July 2018	Morehead
July 2007	Russell Springs		

Insurance

September 1983	Key Insurance Agency	August 2007	Kentucky National Insurance Co.
January 2005	Kentucky Home Life Insurance Co.	December 2017	Mountain Life Insurance Co.
November 2015	Cumberland Valley Insurance		

About the Authors

Gary P. West is a native of Elizabethtown, Kentucky and attended Western Kentucky University before graduating from the University of Kentucky with a journalism degree. For twelve years he was the Executive Director of the Hilltopper Athletic Foundation at WKU and provided color commentary for Wes Strader on the Hilltopper Basketball Network. In 1993, he  became the Executive Director of the Bowling Green Convention & Visitors Bureau. He retired from there in 2006 to devote more time to his writing. This will be his twelfth book.

Eddie Woodruff is Chief Marketing & Communications Officer for the Forcht Group of Kentucky. Woodruff is originally from Morganfield, Kentucky, and holds a B.A. Degree in Communications from Western Kentucky University and a Master's Degree in Management from Brescia University. He began working for Terry Forcht in 2007 after a career as a radio station General Manager, bank Marketing Director, and the Co-Owner of an advertising and public relations agency in Evansville, IN. His insider knowledge gained from working with Terry Forcht on a daily basis gives readers a unique perspective on the man and his businesses.

Index